This Book Belongs To

_____

_____

_____

Letters & Numbers Tracing
Publisher: Inner Vitality Systems, LLC.
Website: www.InnerVitalitySystems.com
ISBN: 978-1-951382-09-4

Copyright © 2020 by Inner Vitality Systems, LLC
All rights reserved. No part of this publication may be reproduced or utilized in any form or by any means, electronic or mechanical, including photocopying, recording, or by any information storage and retrieval system, without prior written permission from the publisher. All rights reserved including the right of reproduction in whole or in part in any form. Inquiries should be addressed to the publisher.

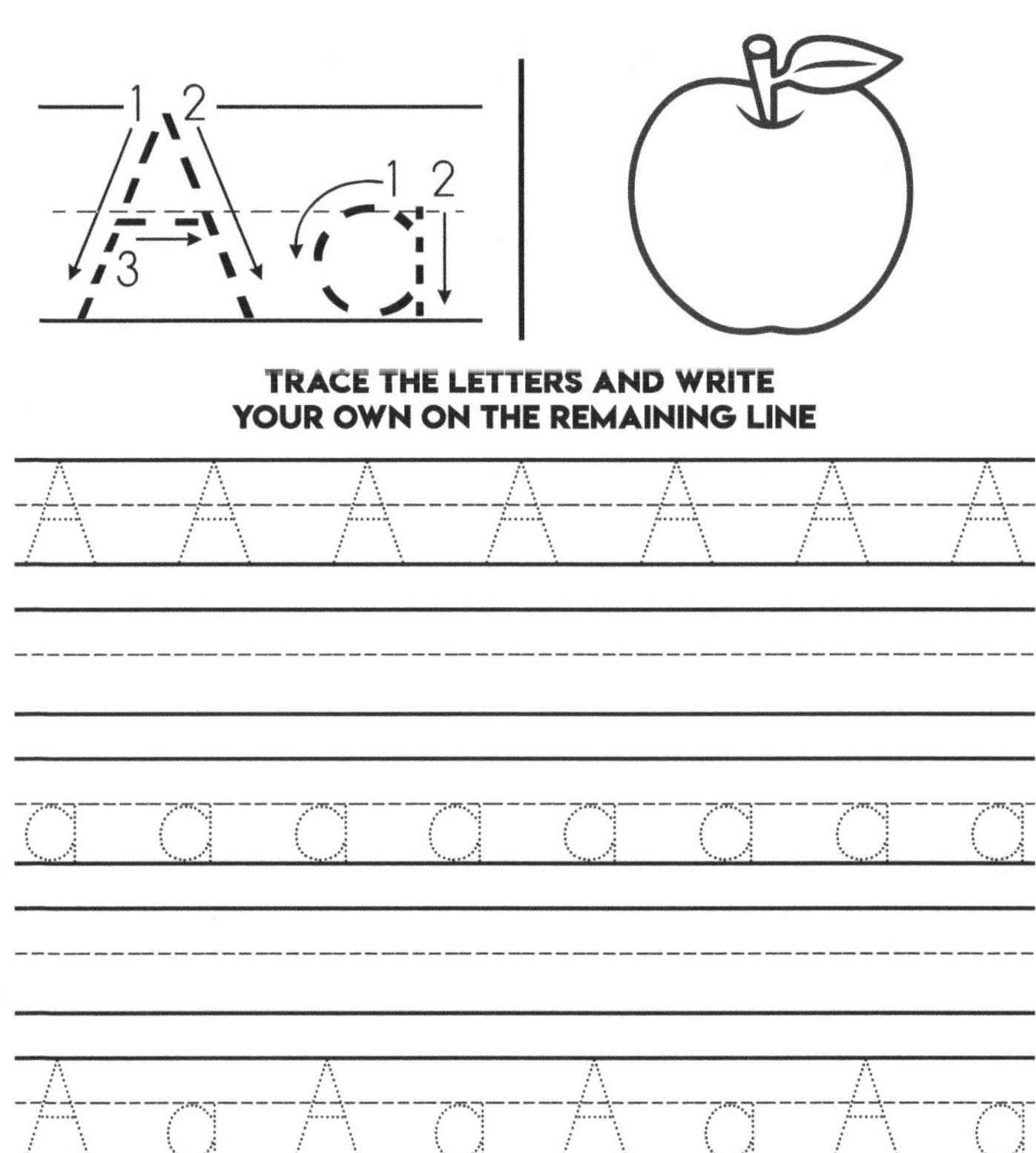

TRACE THE LETTERS AND WRITE YOUR OWN ON THE REMAINING LINE

aaaaaaa

aaaaaaa

aaaaaaa

aaaaaaa

aaaaaaa

cccccc

cccccc

cccccc

cccccc

cccccc

cccccc

c c c c c c c

c c c c c c c

c c c c c c c

c c c c c c c

c c c c c c c

c c c c c c c

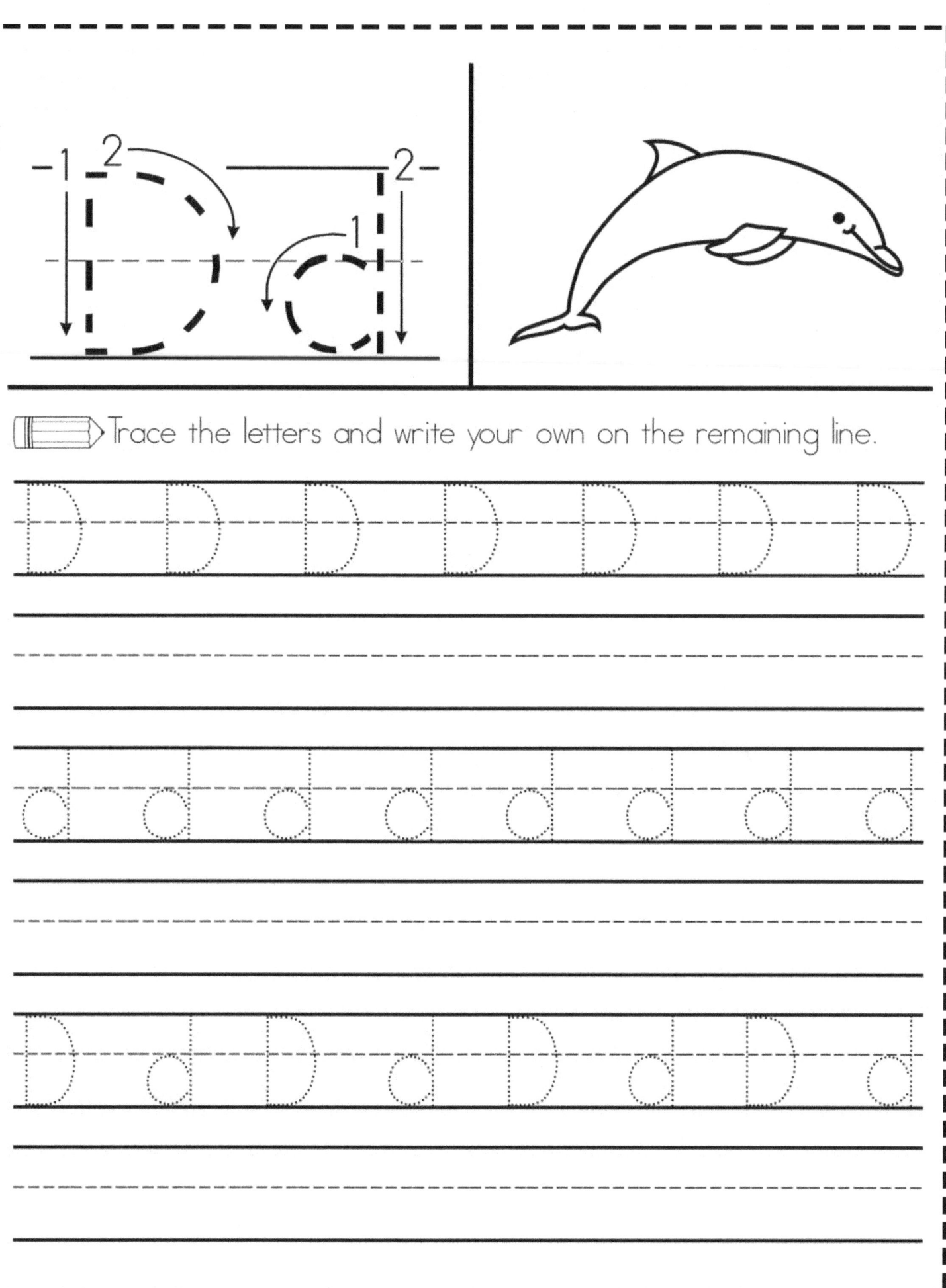

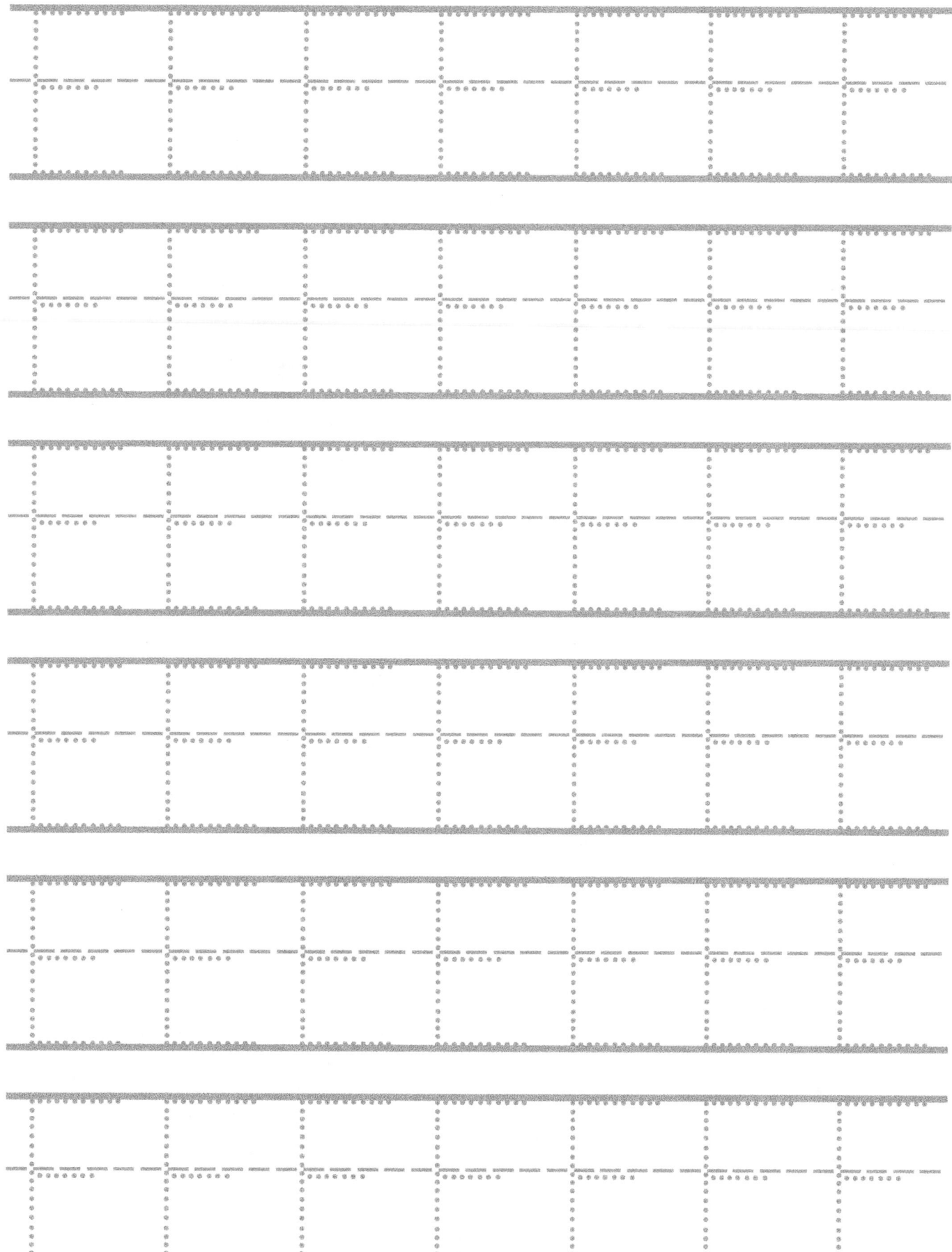

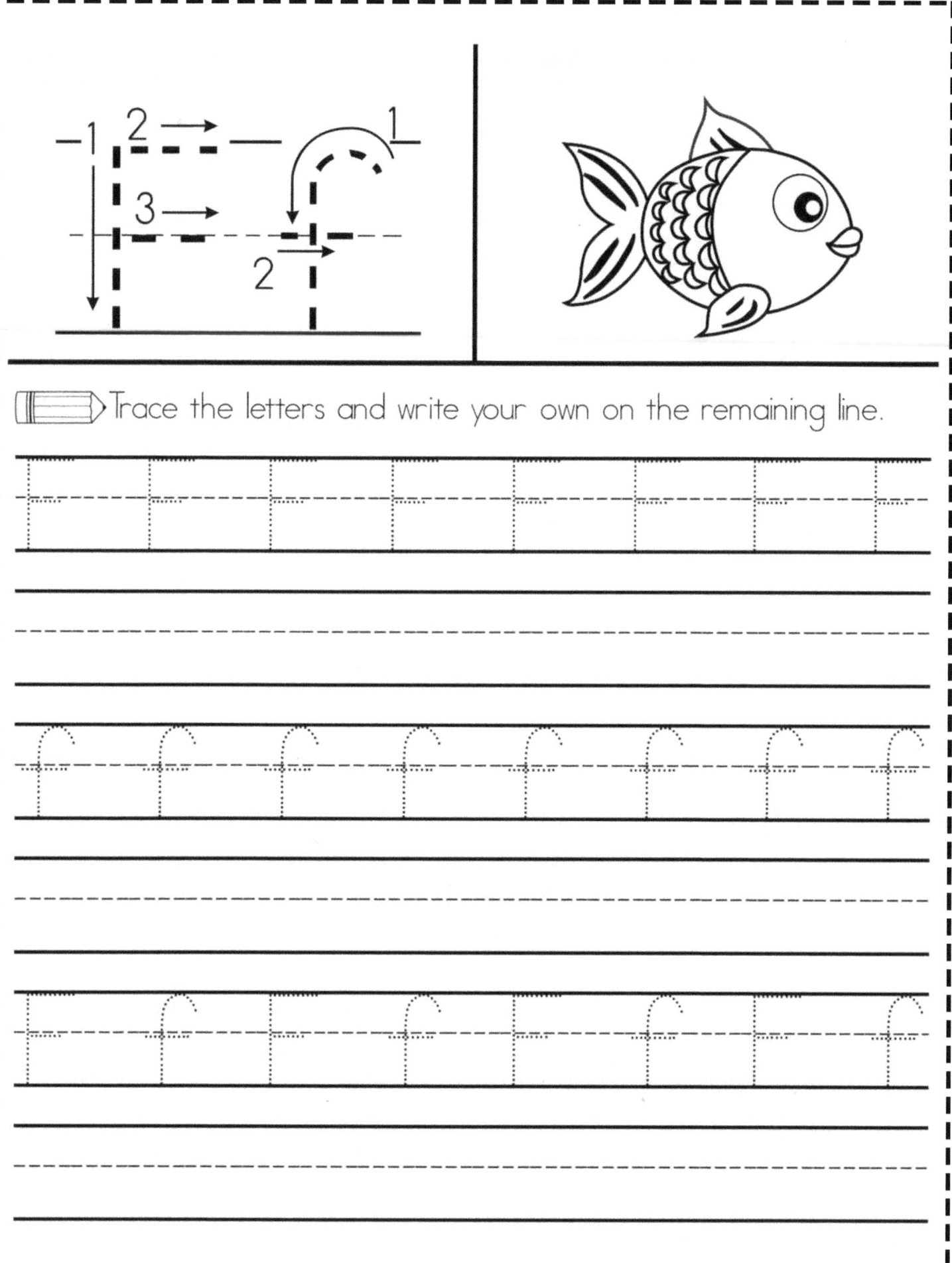

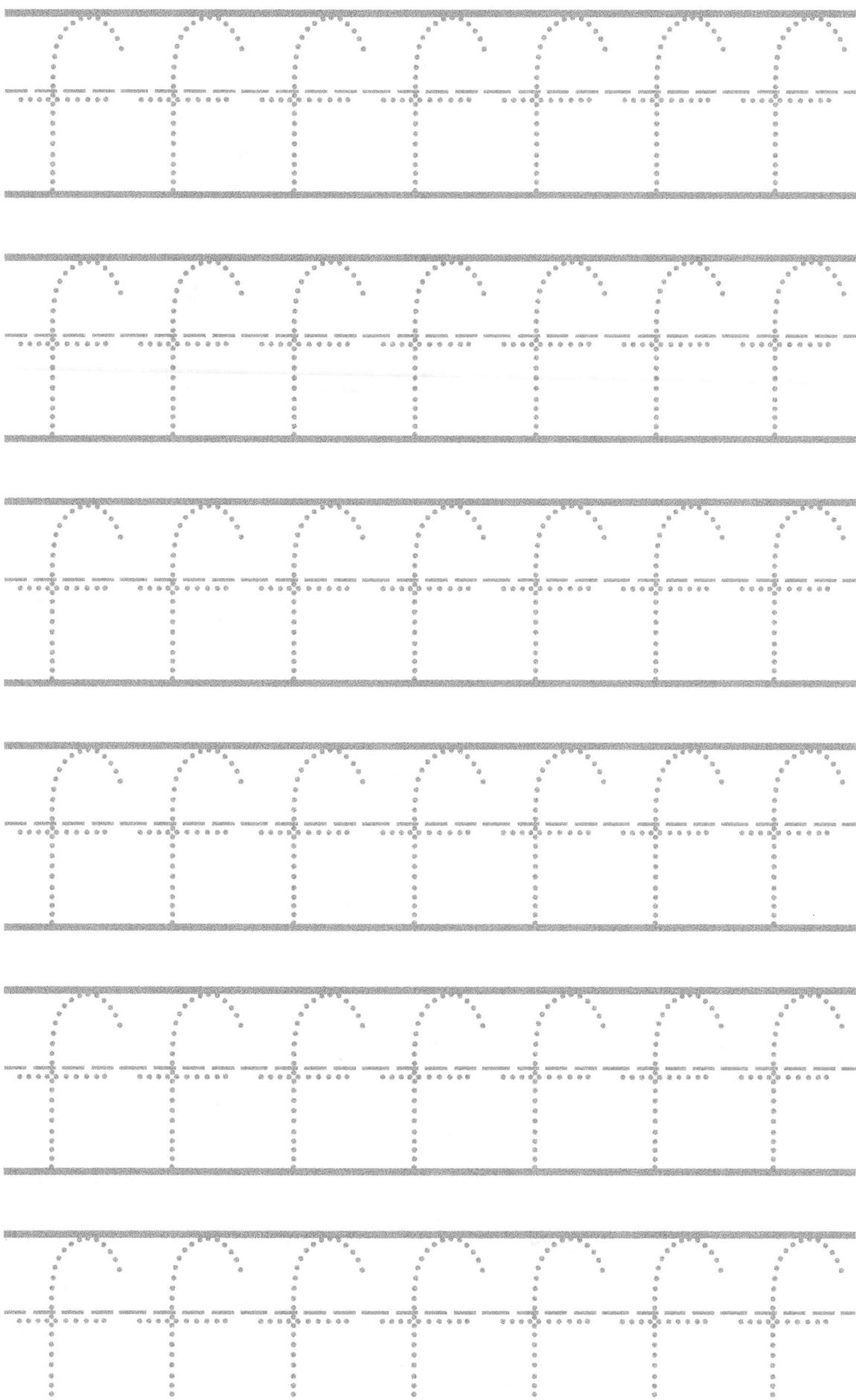

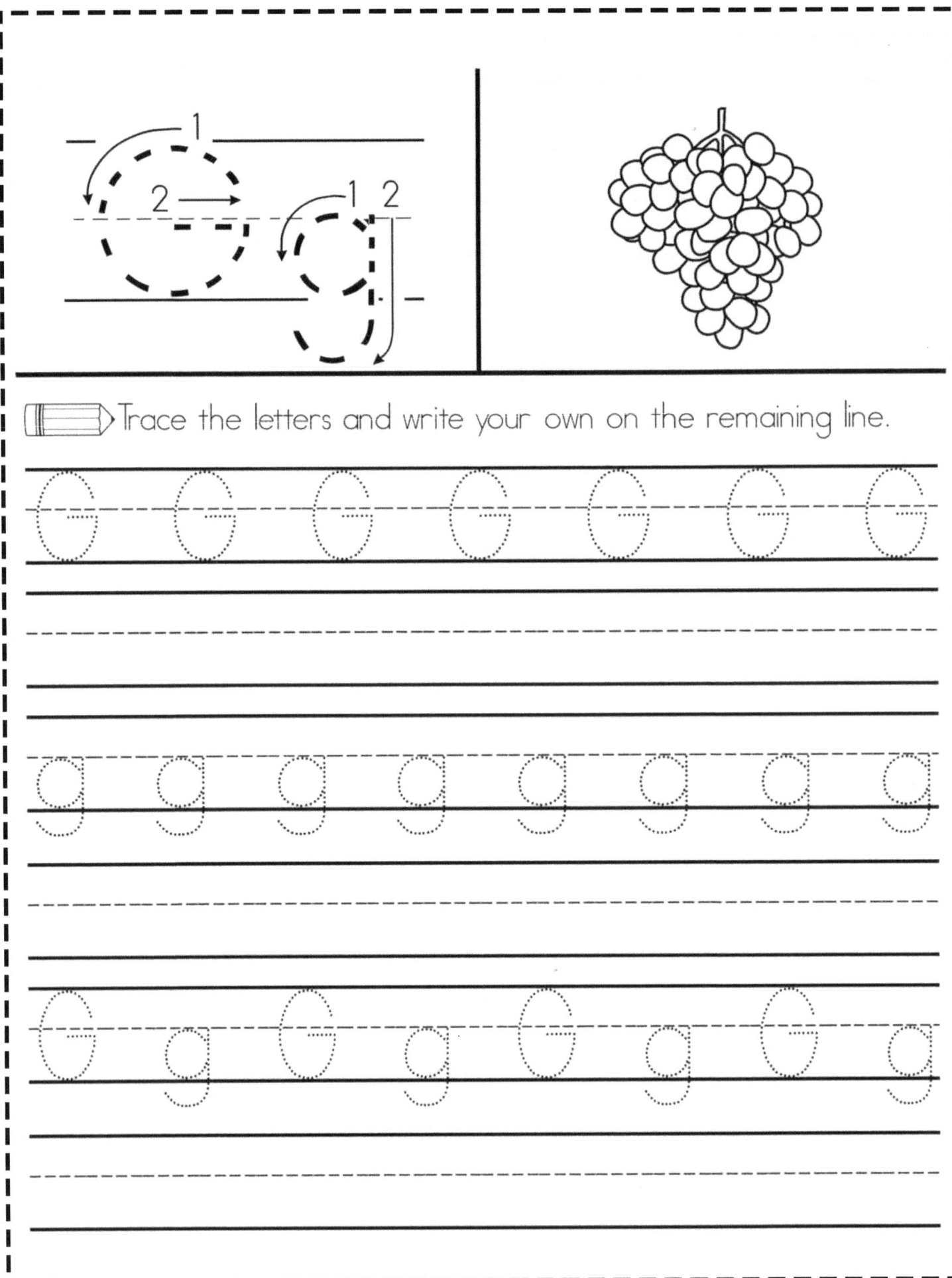

GGGGGGG

GGGGGGG

GGGGGGG

GGGGGGG

GGGGGGG

GGGGGGG

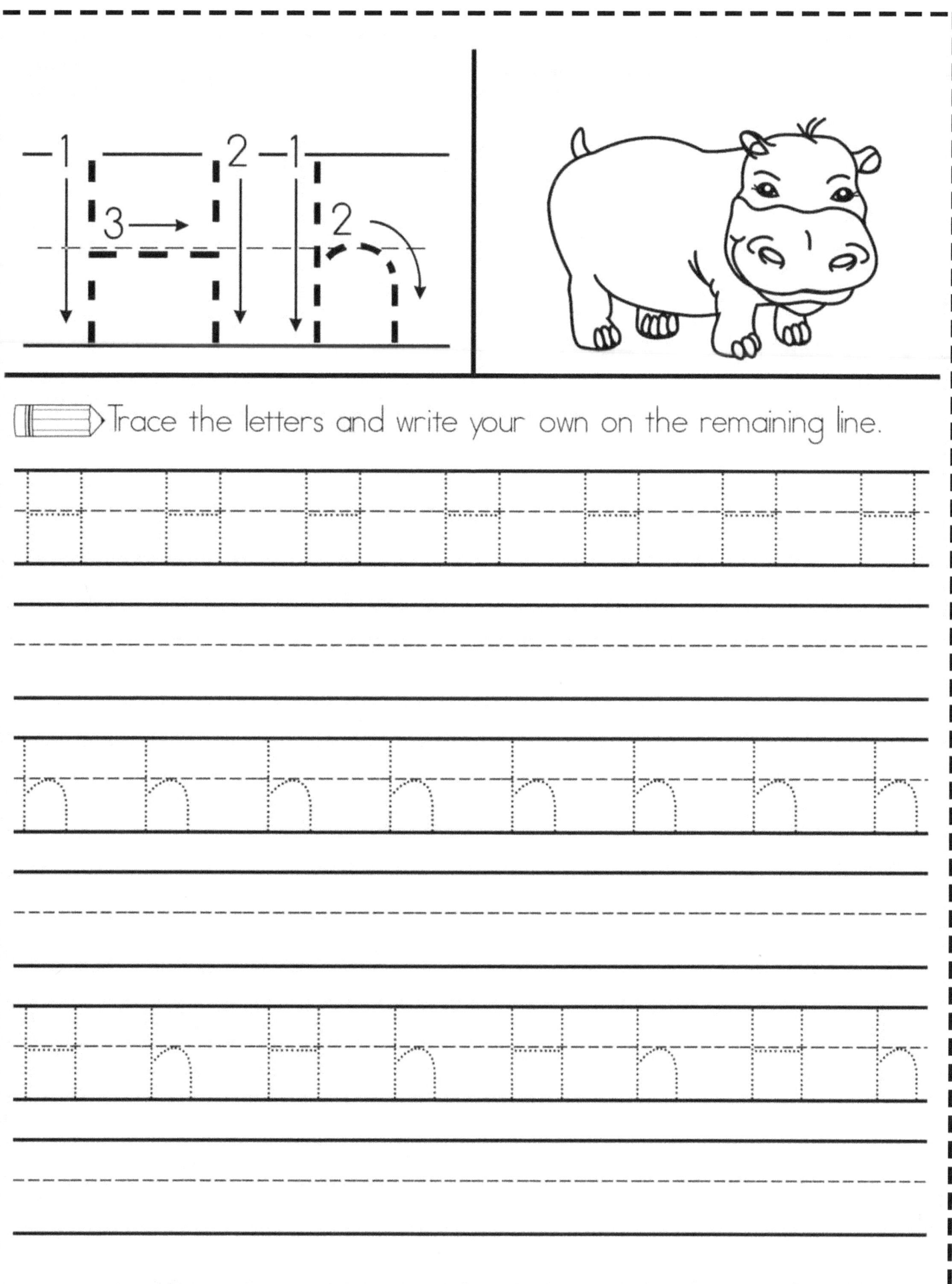

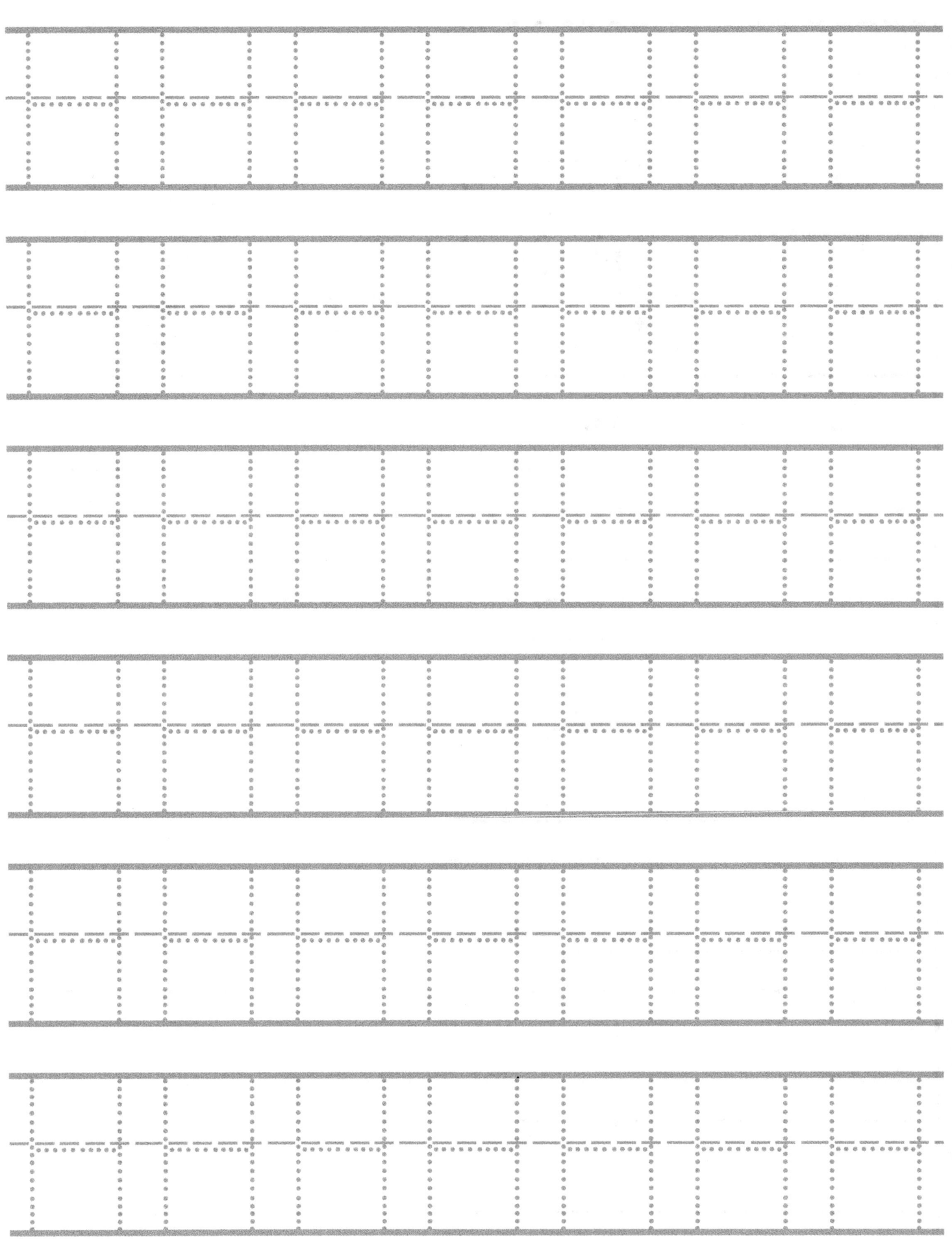

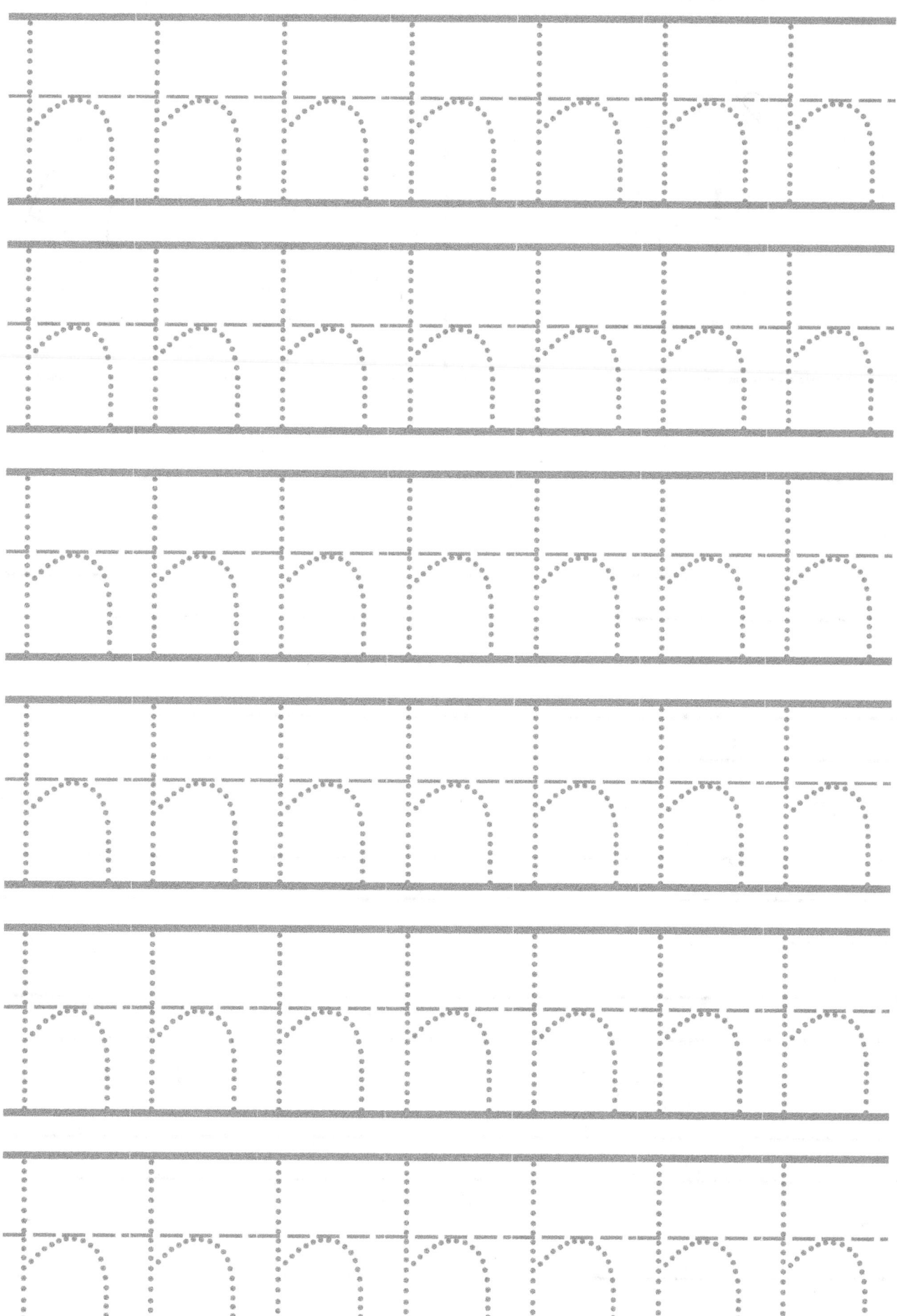

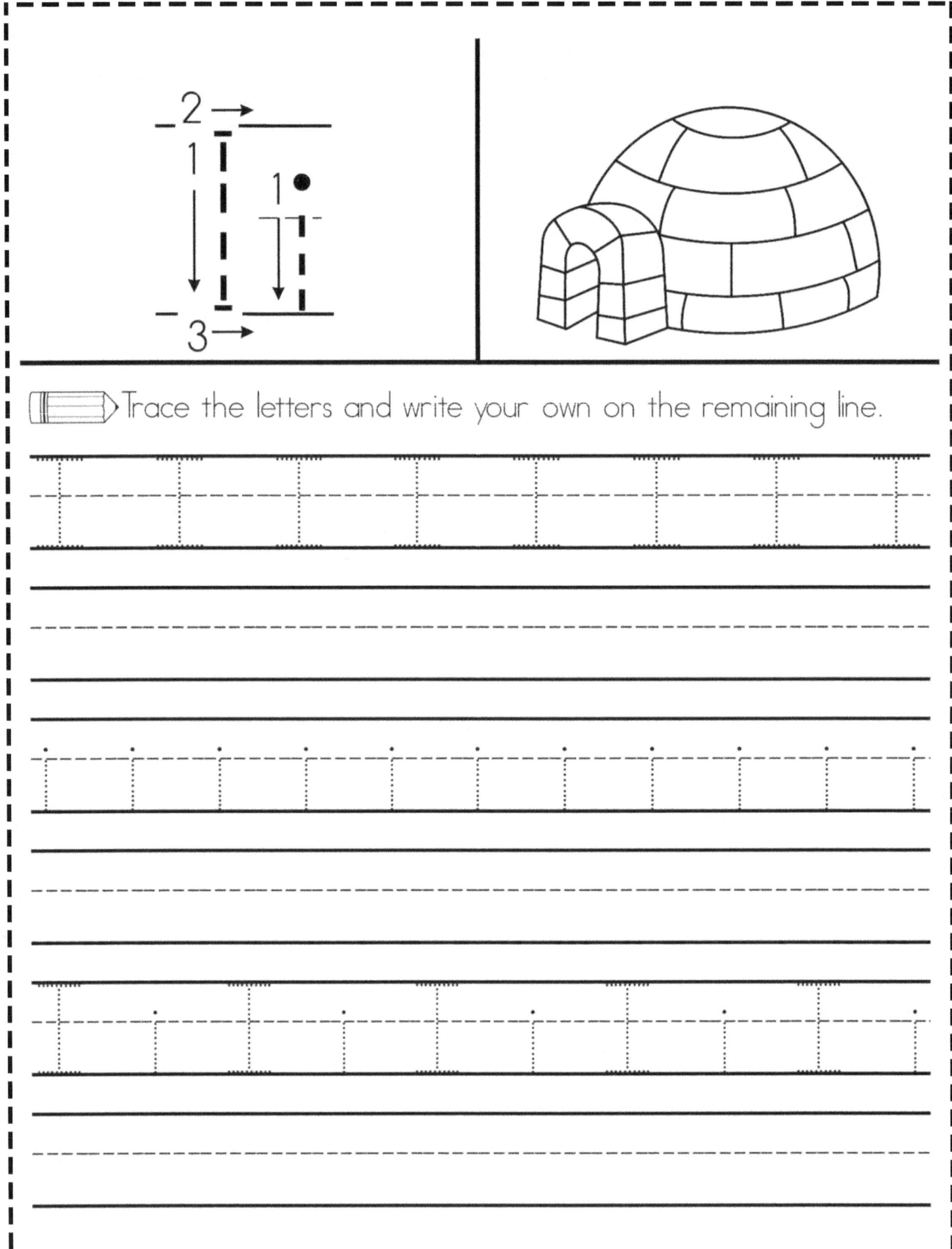

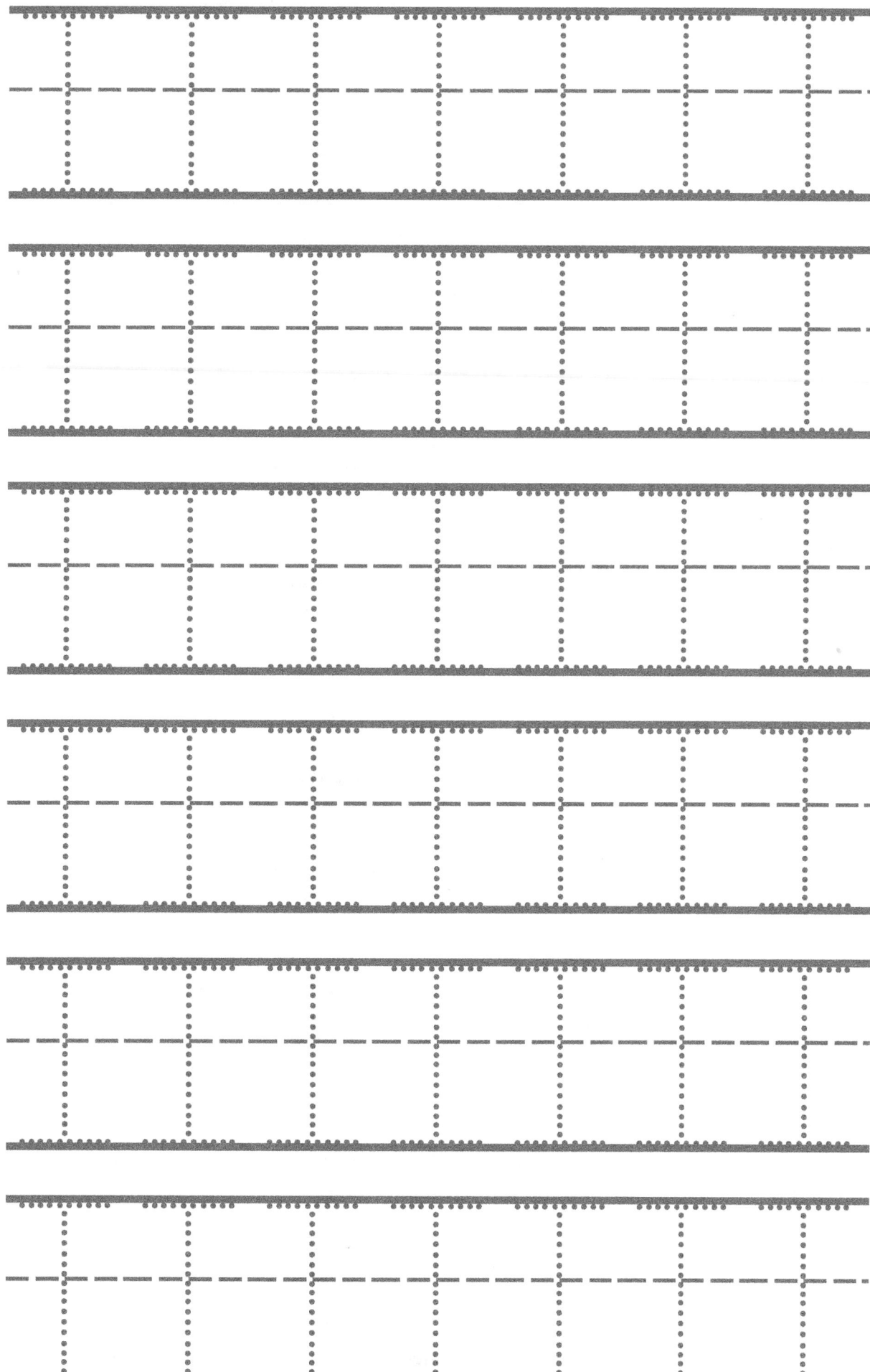

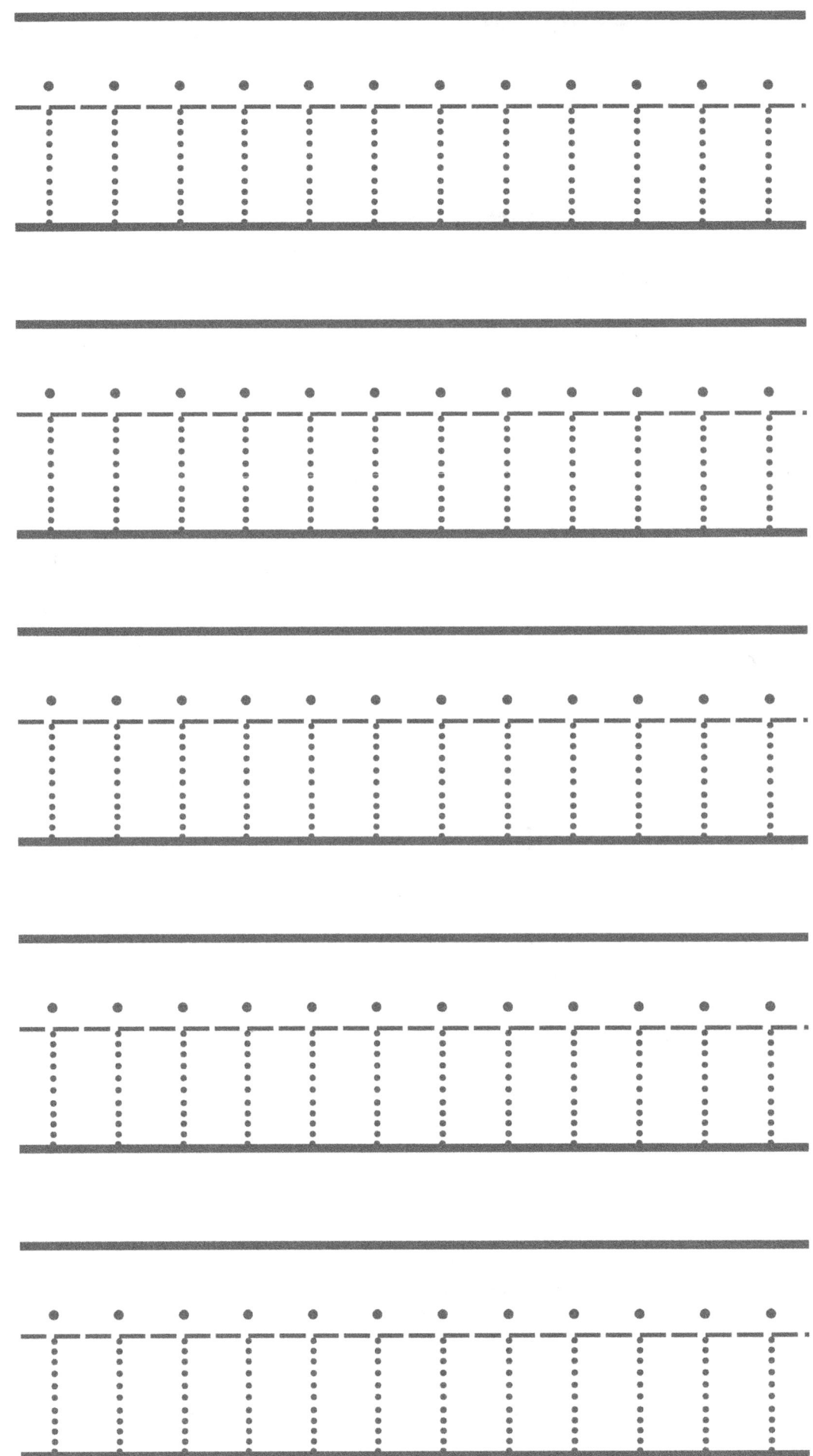

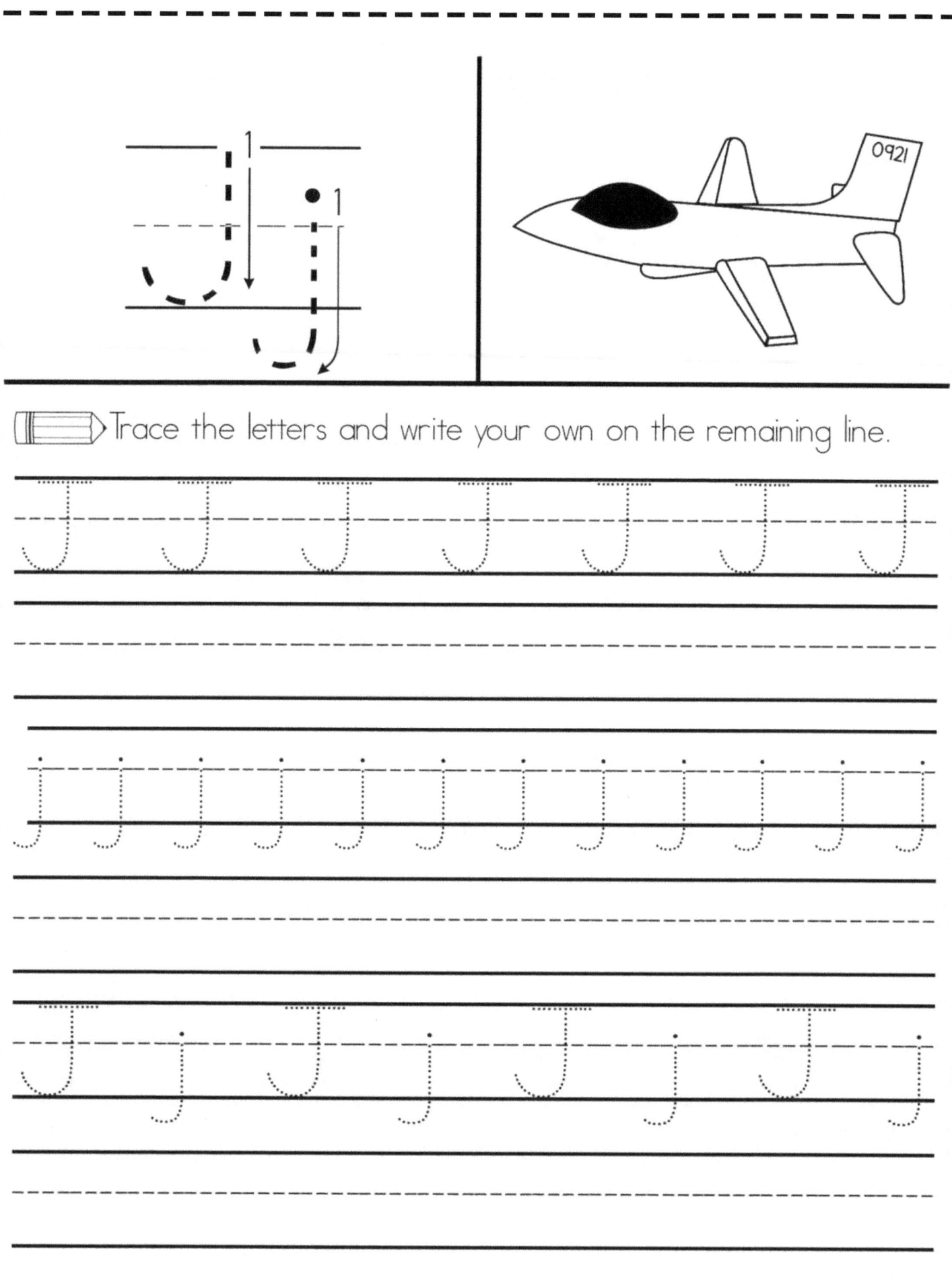

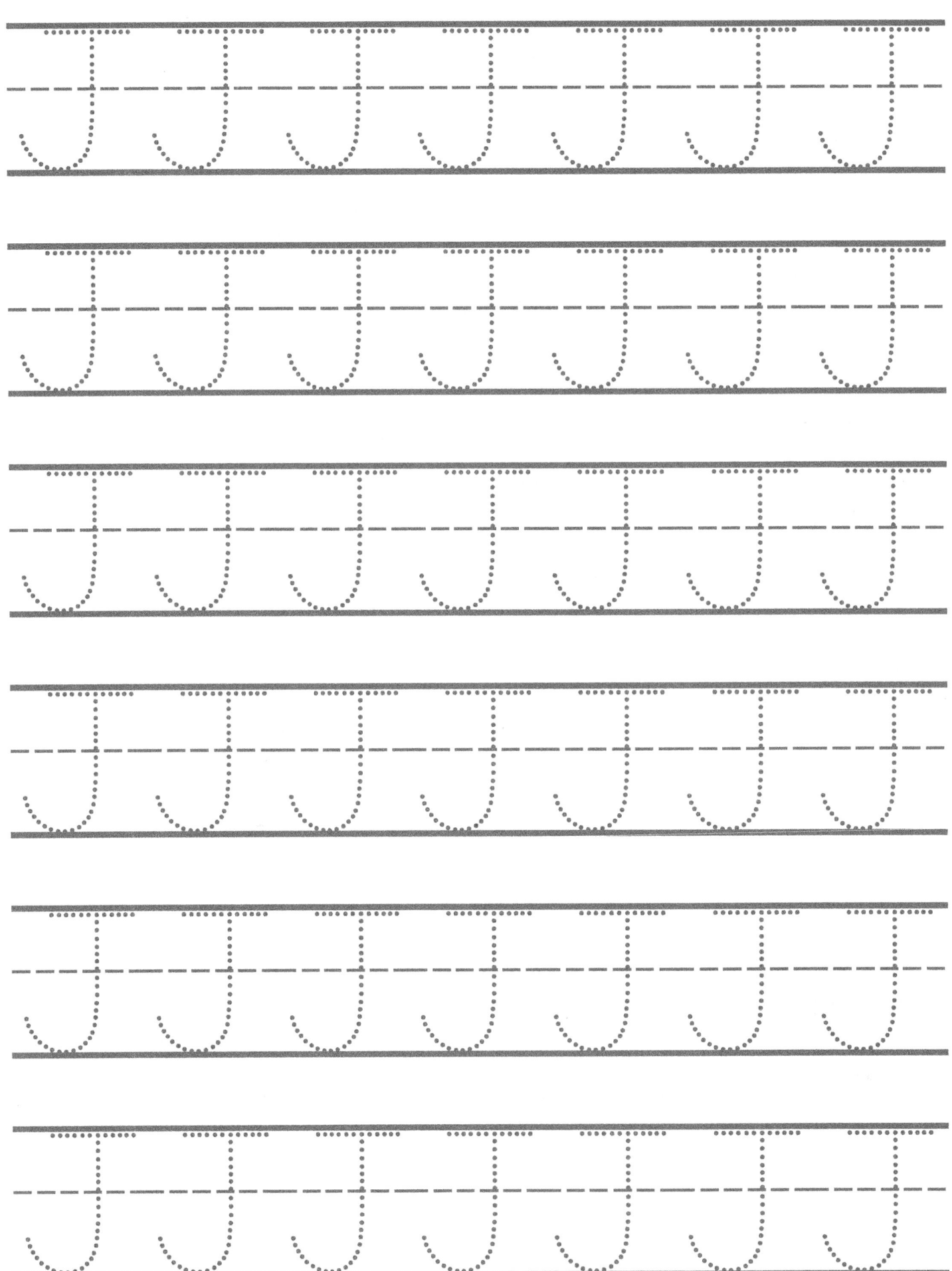

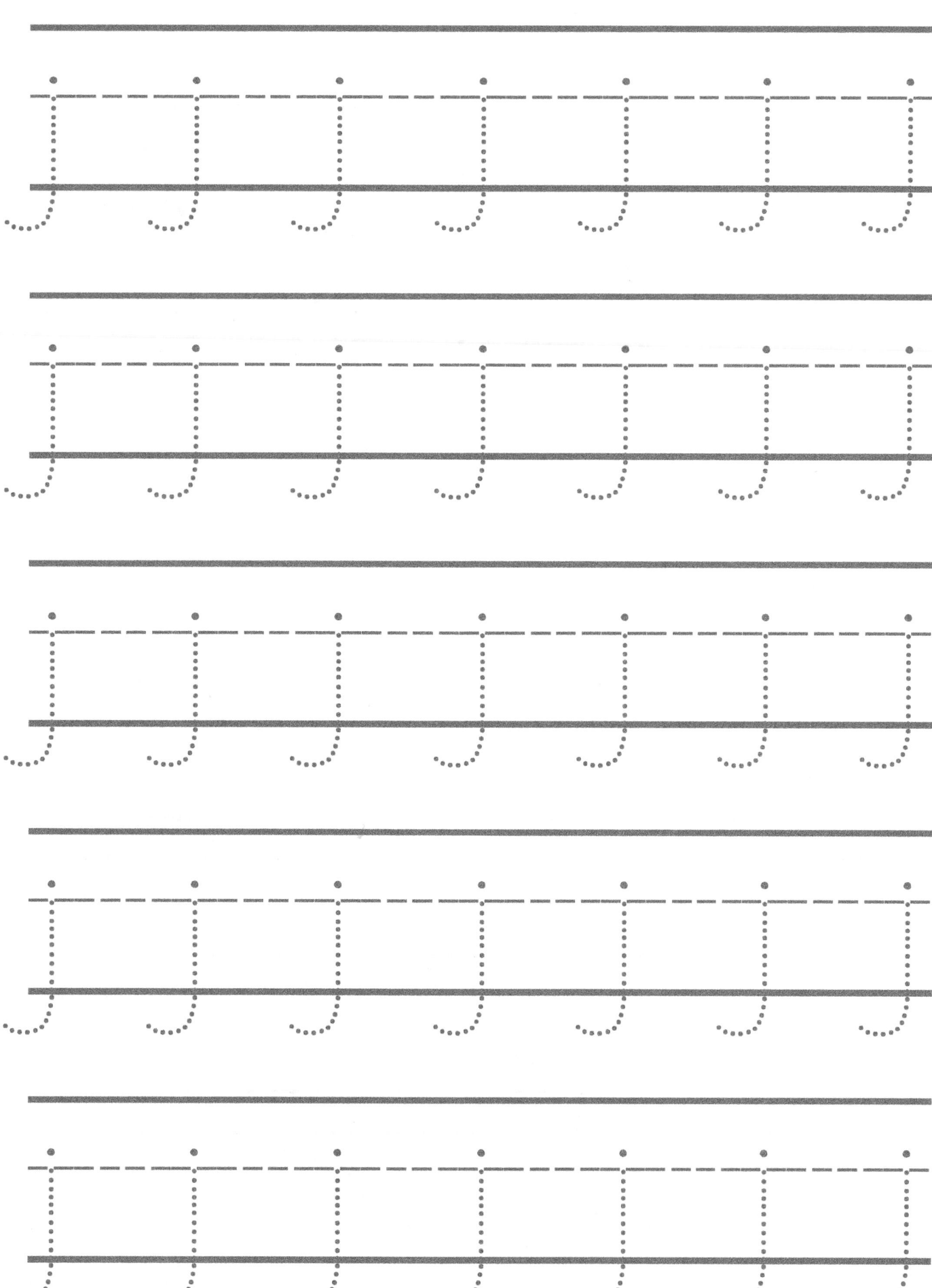

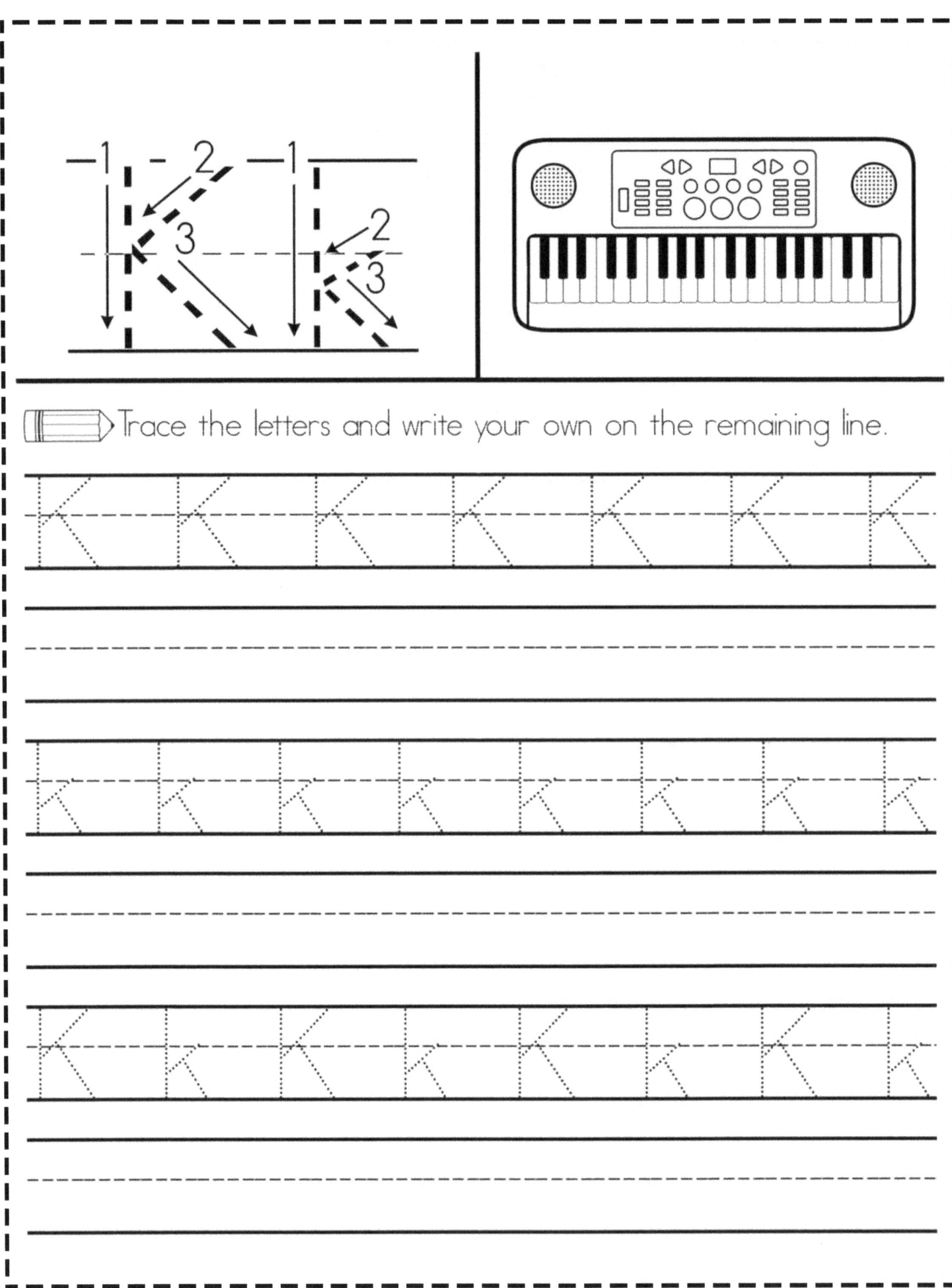

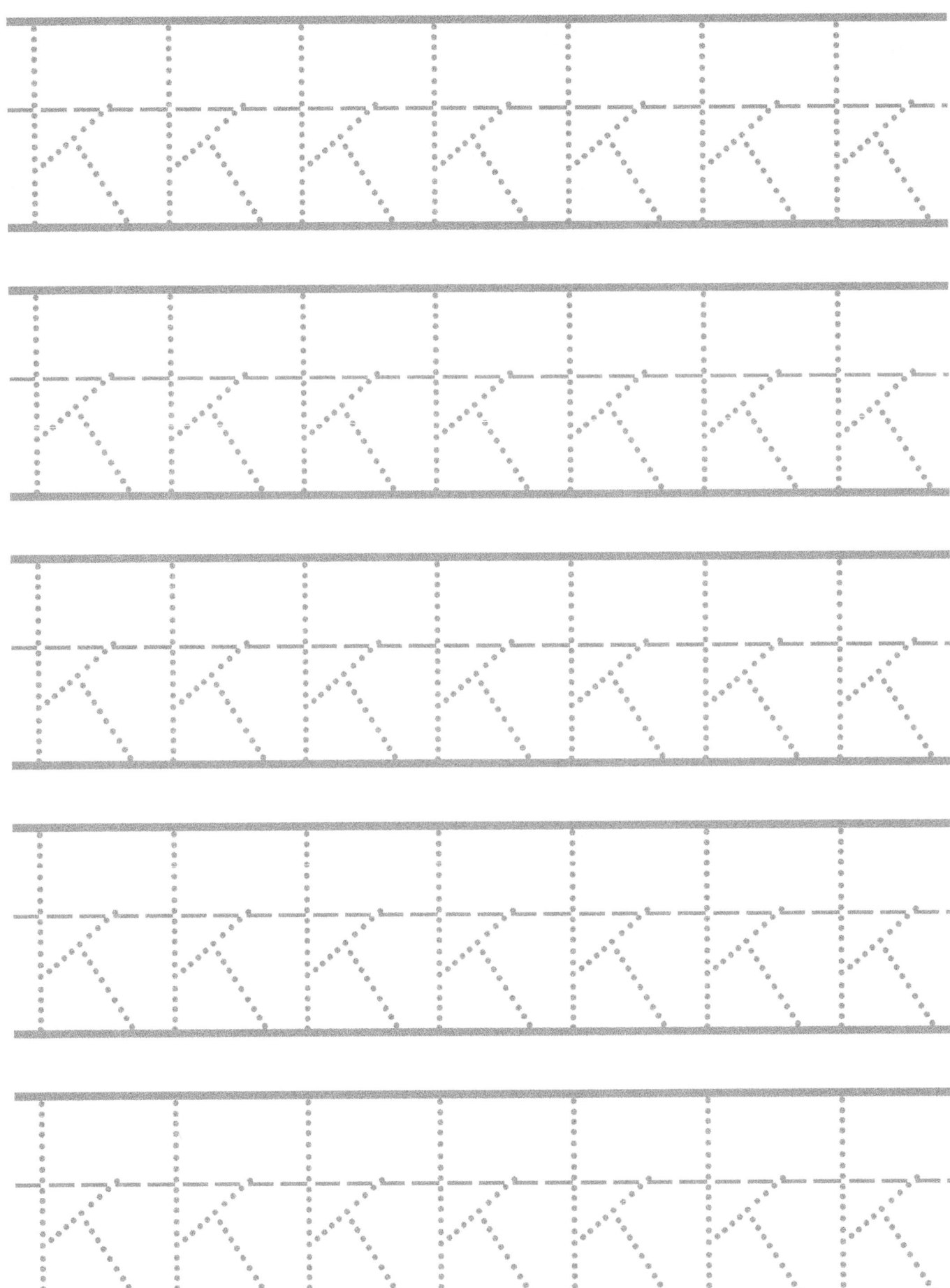

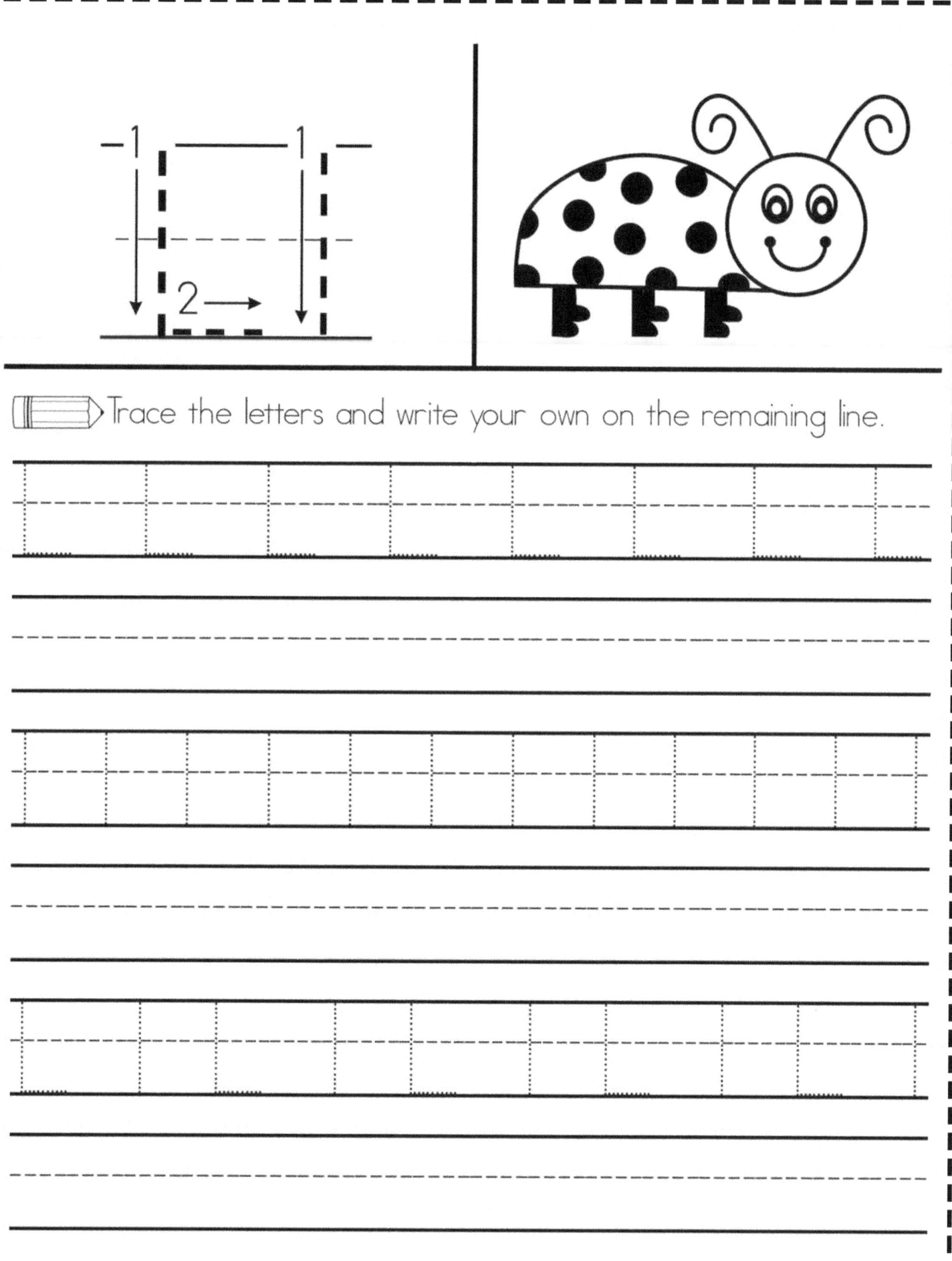

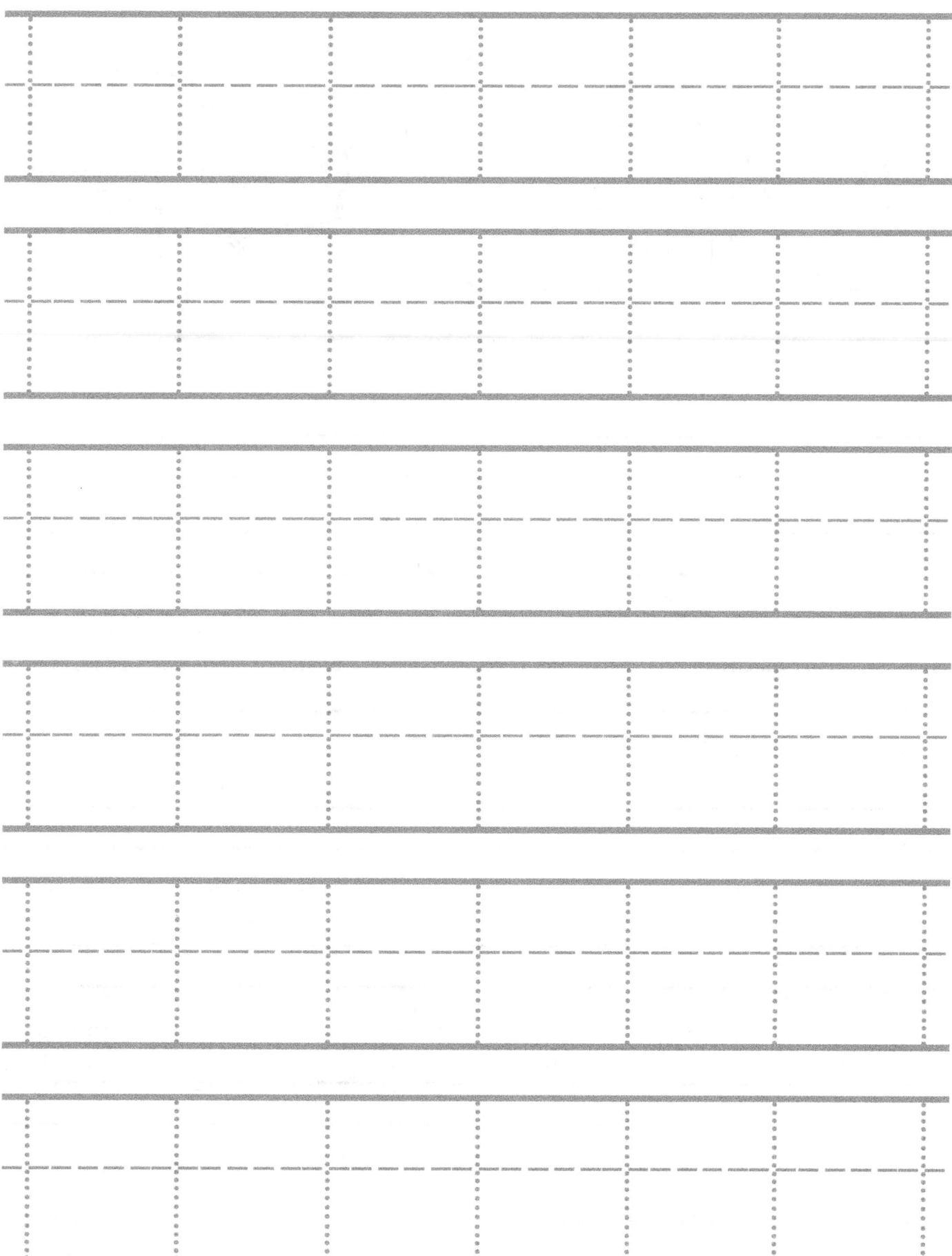

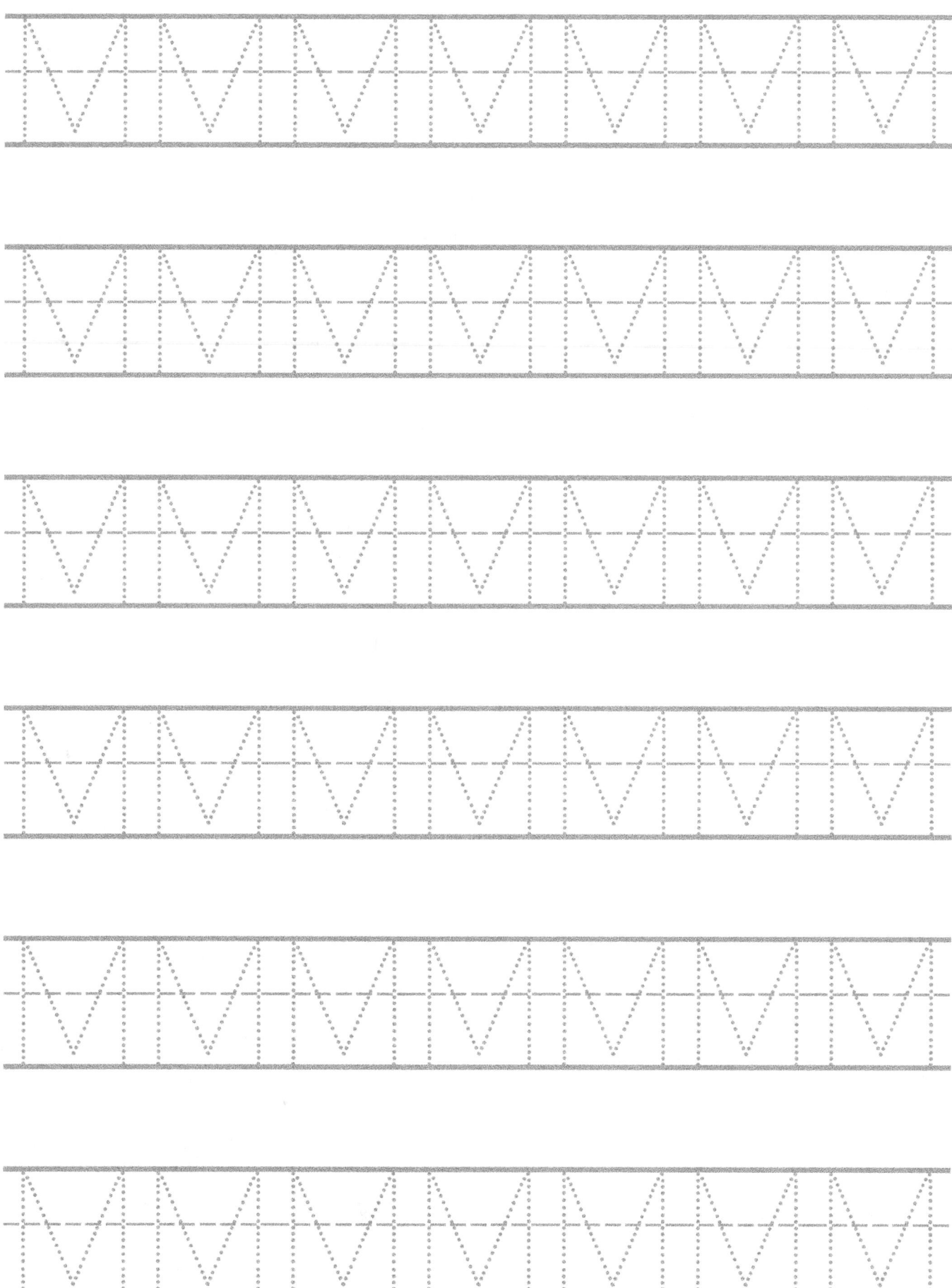

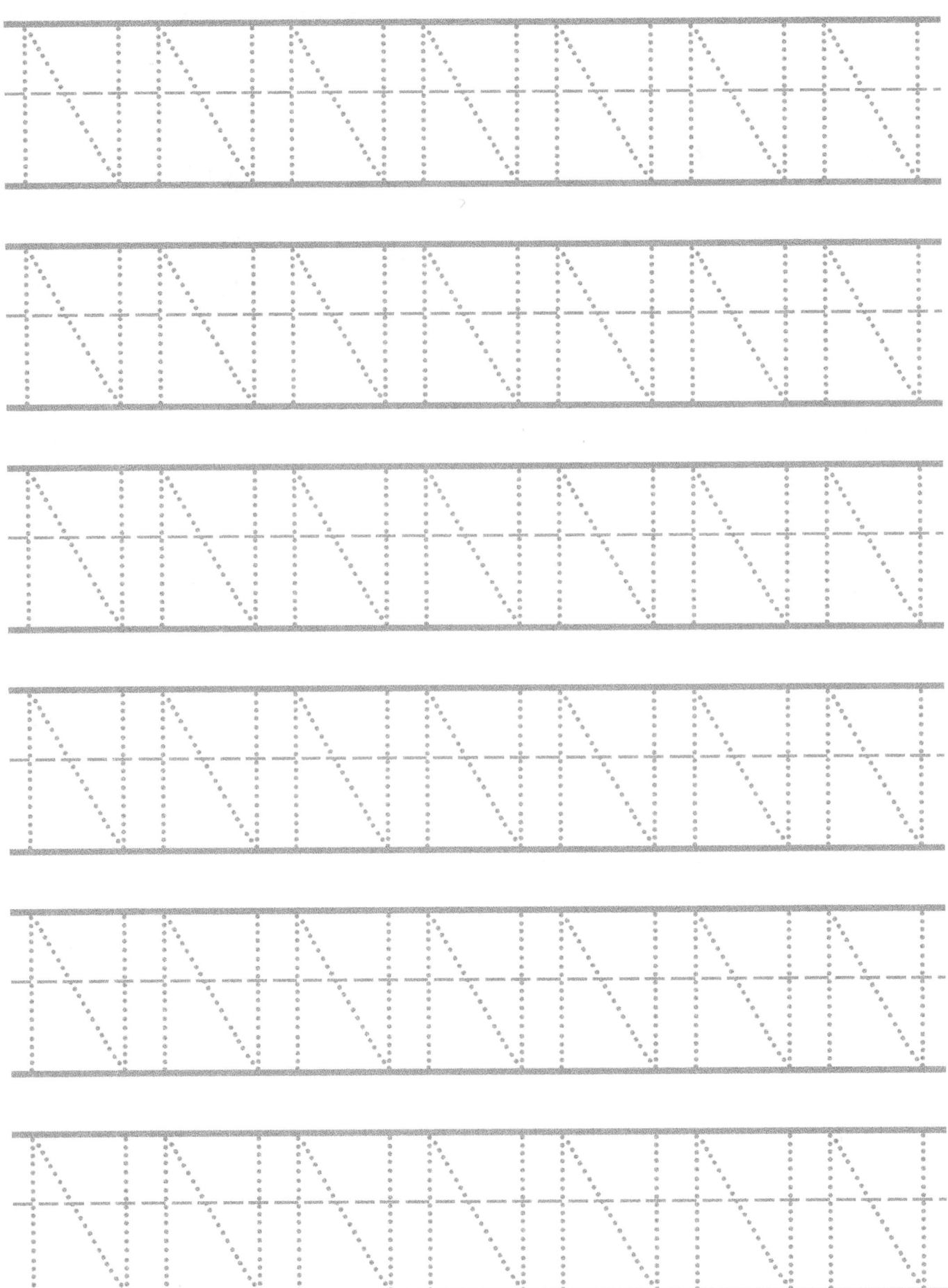

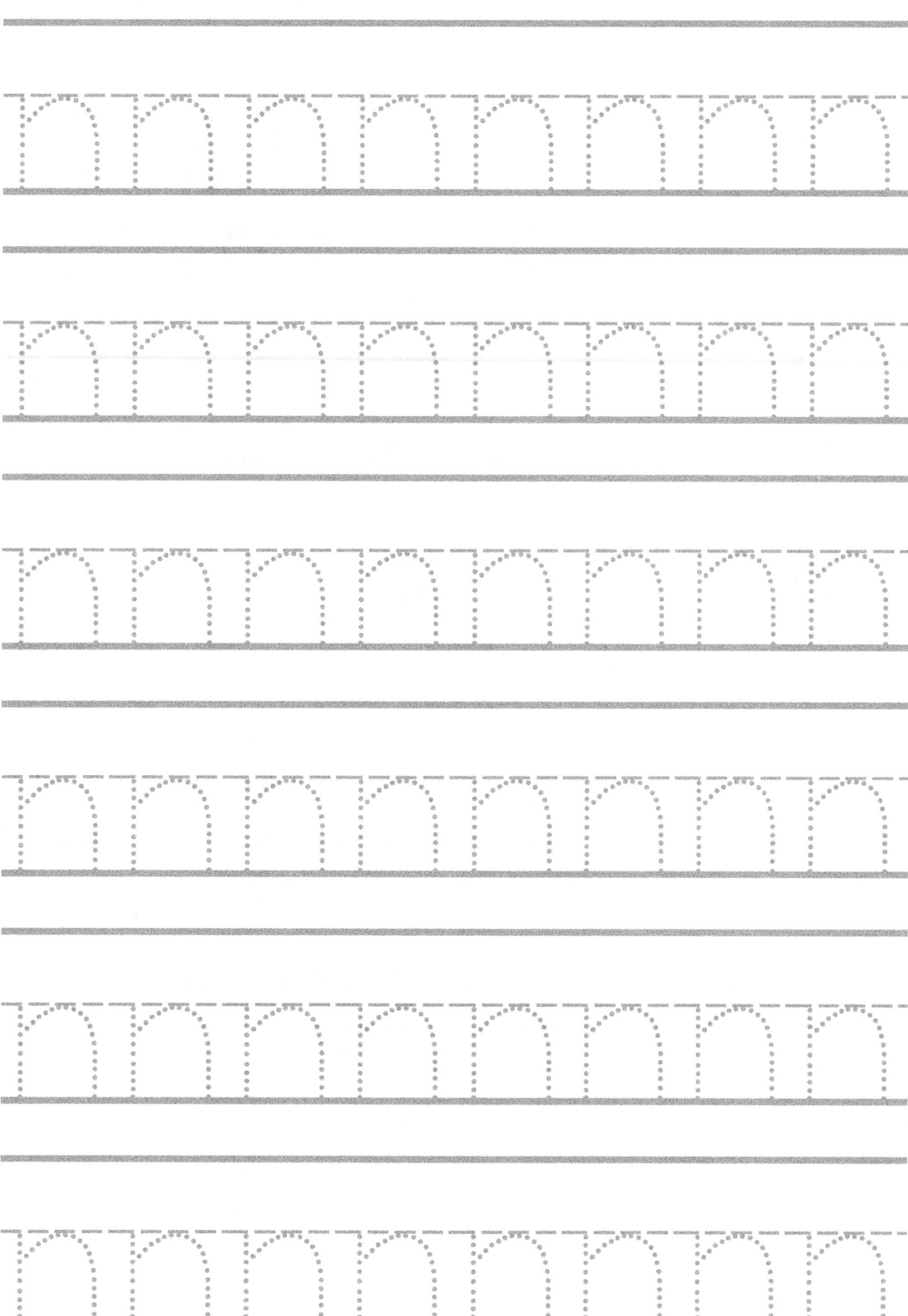

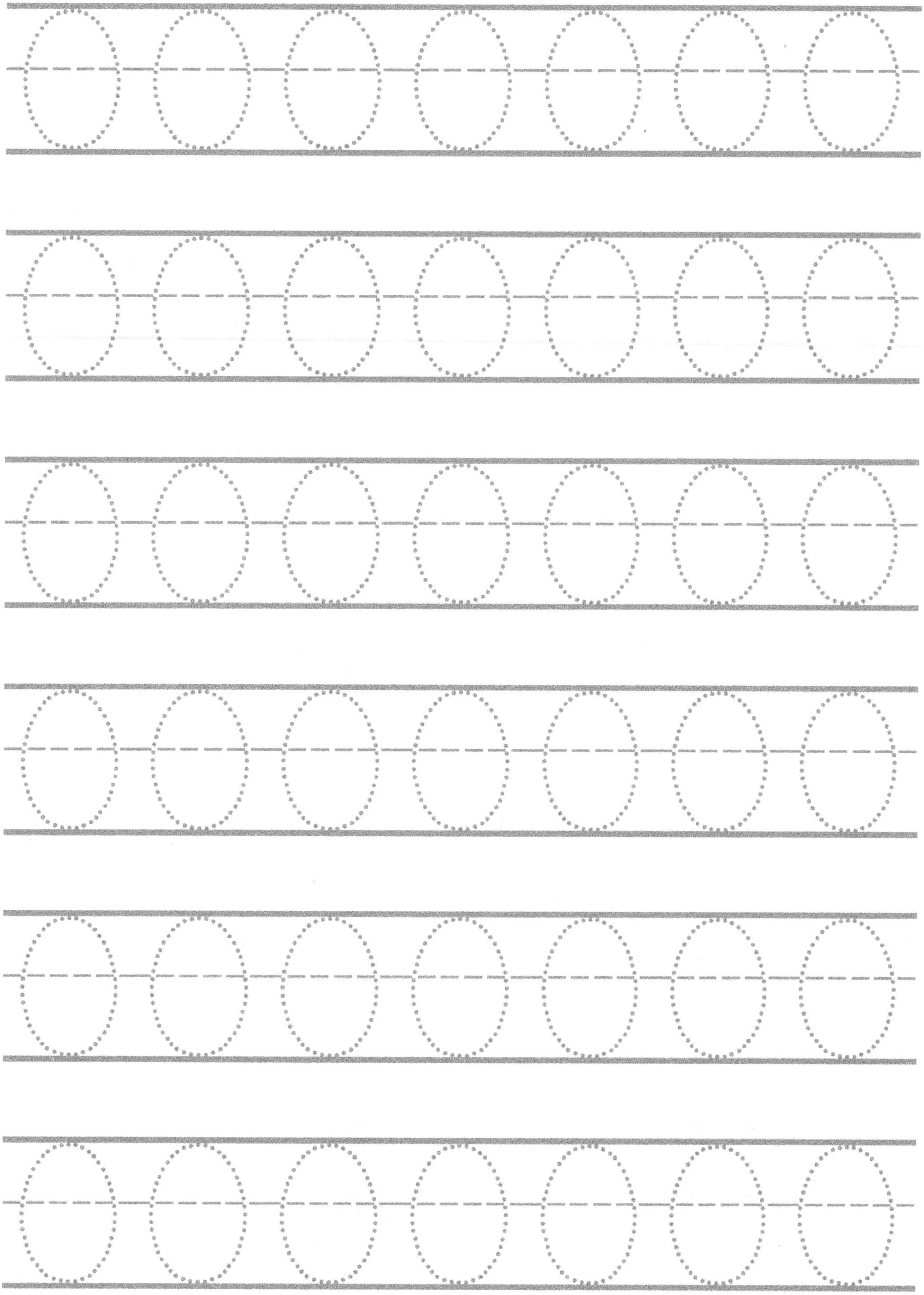

p p p p p p p

p p p p p p p

p p p p p p p

p p p p p p p

p p p p p p p

p p p p p p p

p p p p p p p

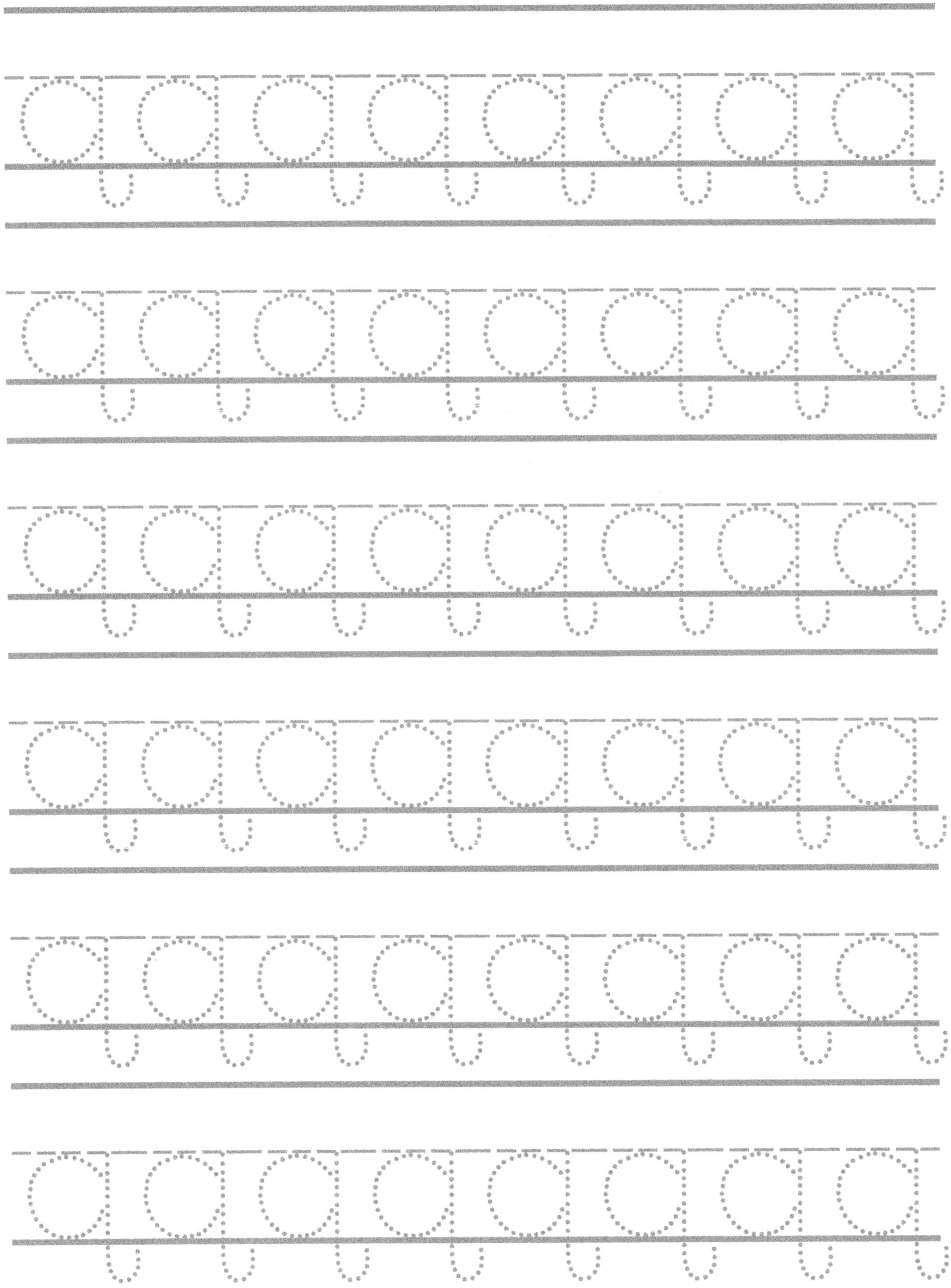

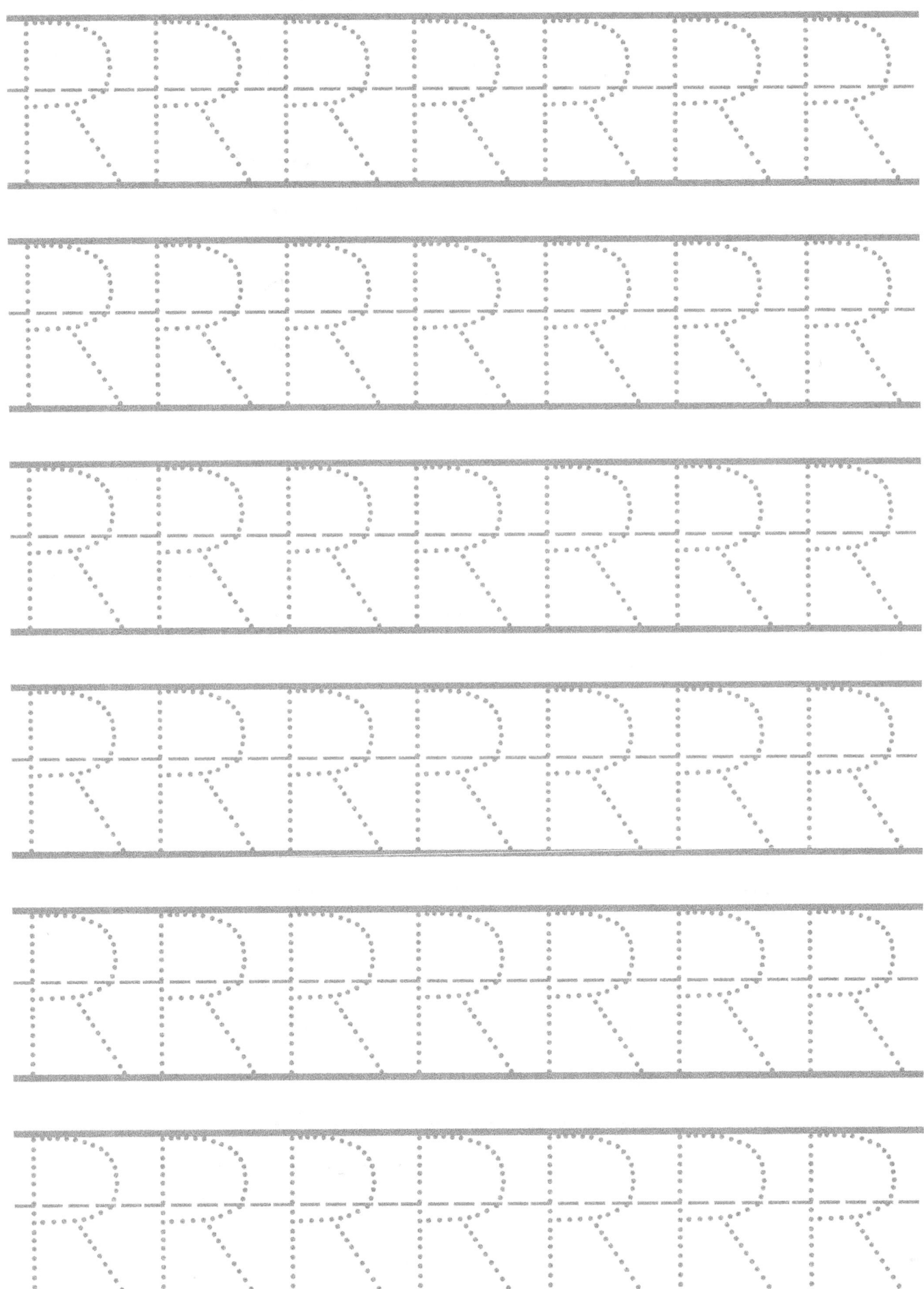

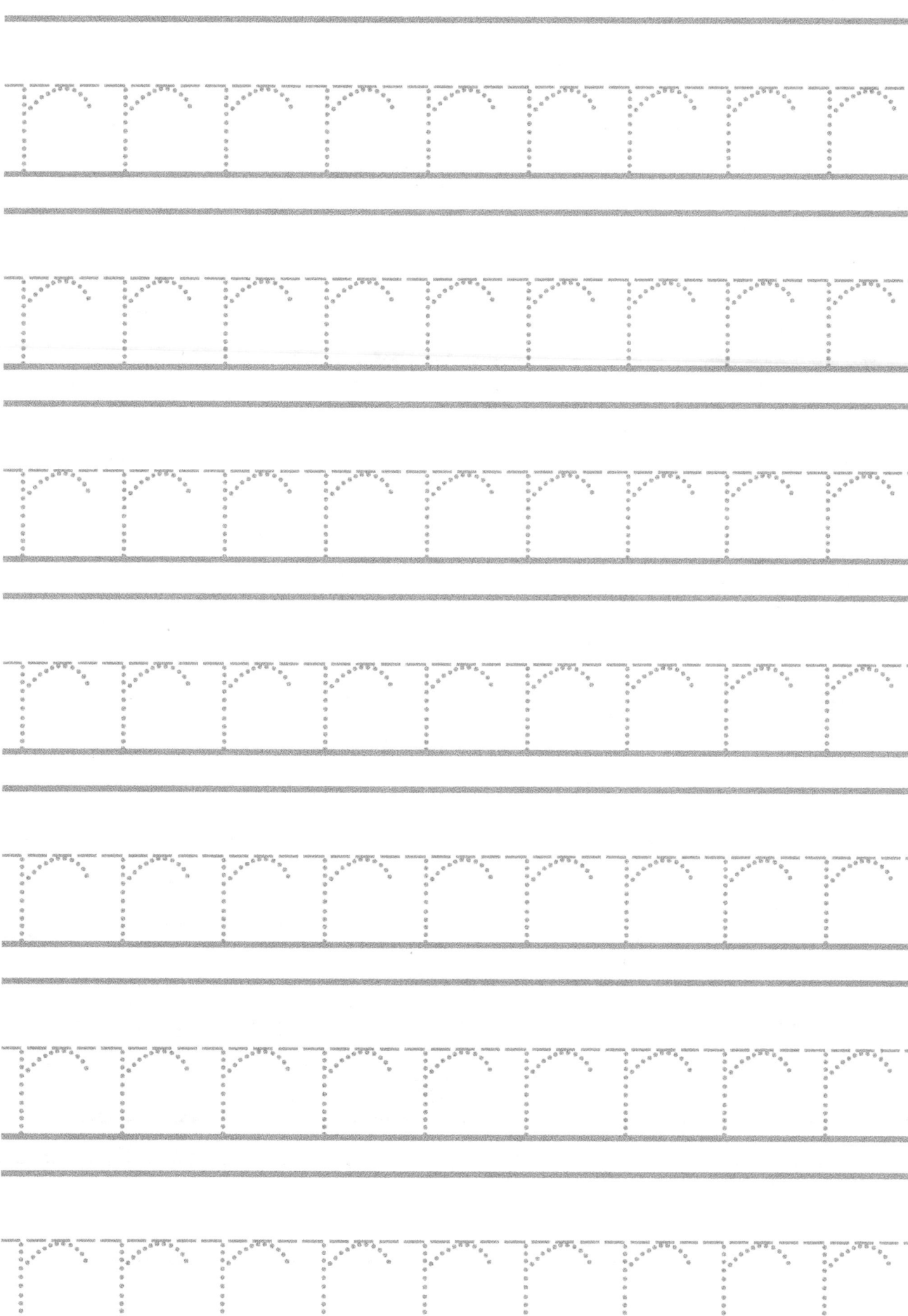

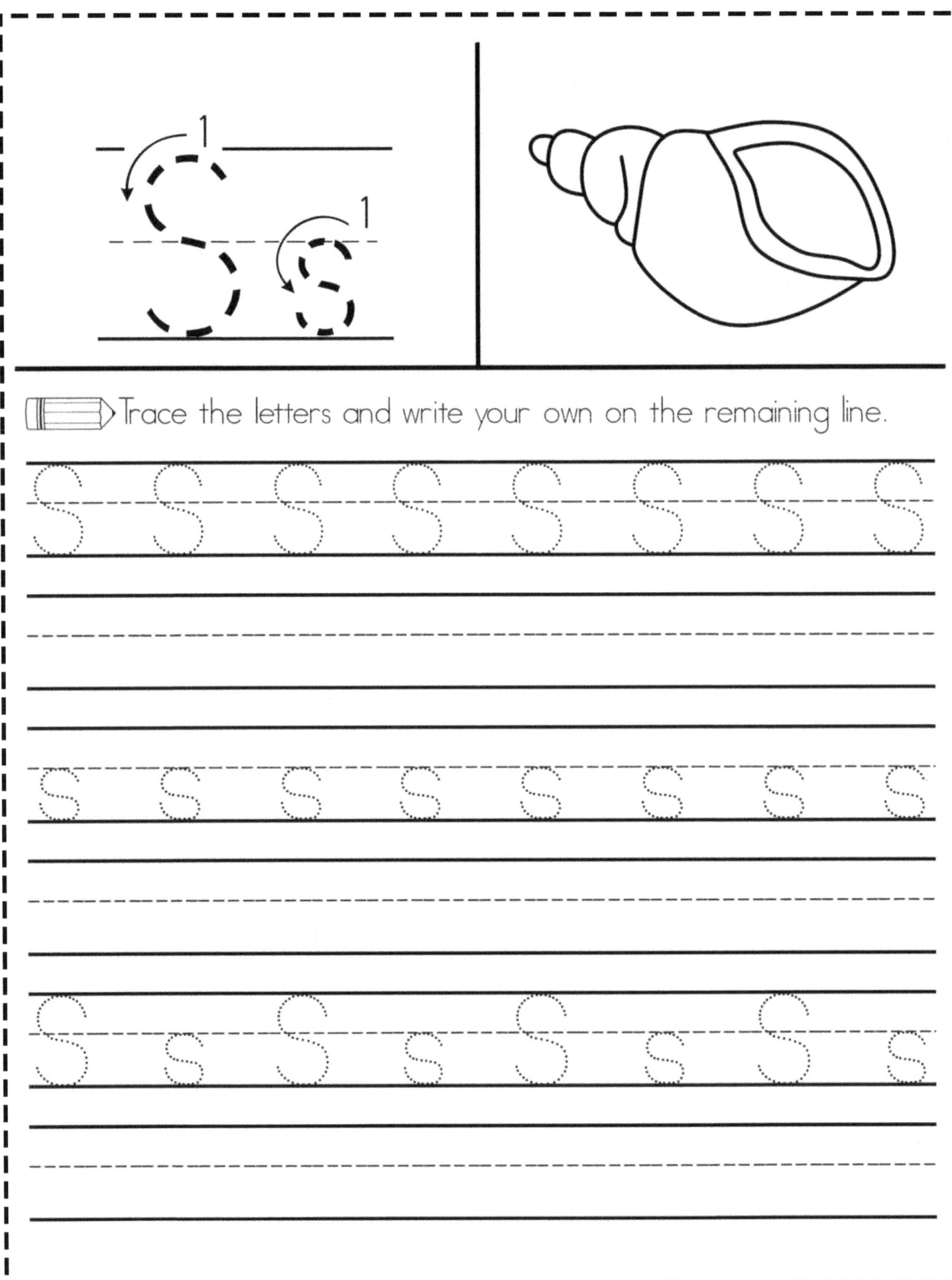

SSSSSSSS
SSSSSSSS
SSSSSSSS
SSSSSSSS
SSSSSSSS
SSSSSSSS

SSSSSSSSS

SSSSSSSSS

SSSSSSSSS

SSSSSSSSS

SSSSSSSSS

SSSSSSSSS

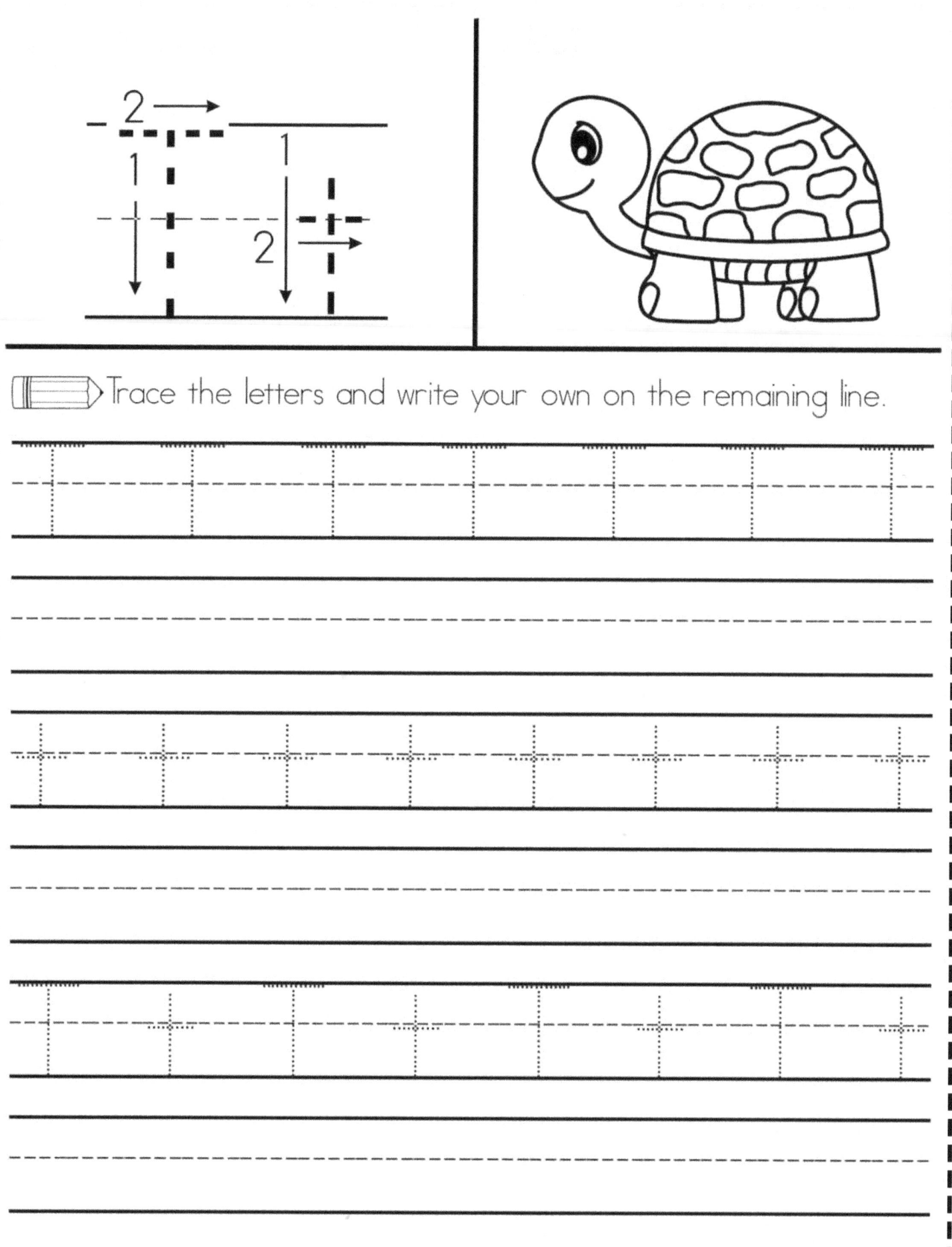

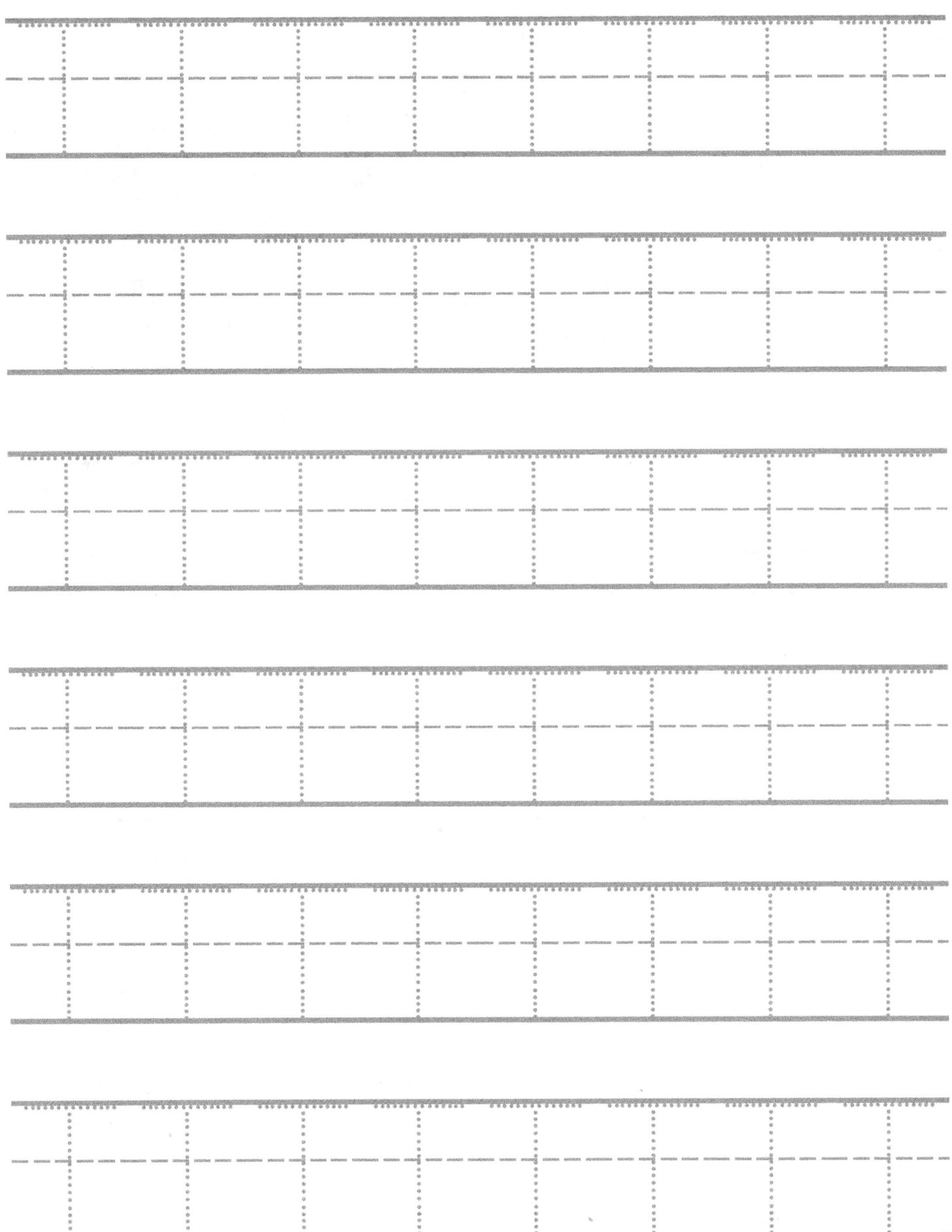

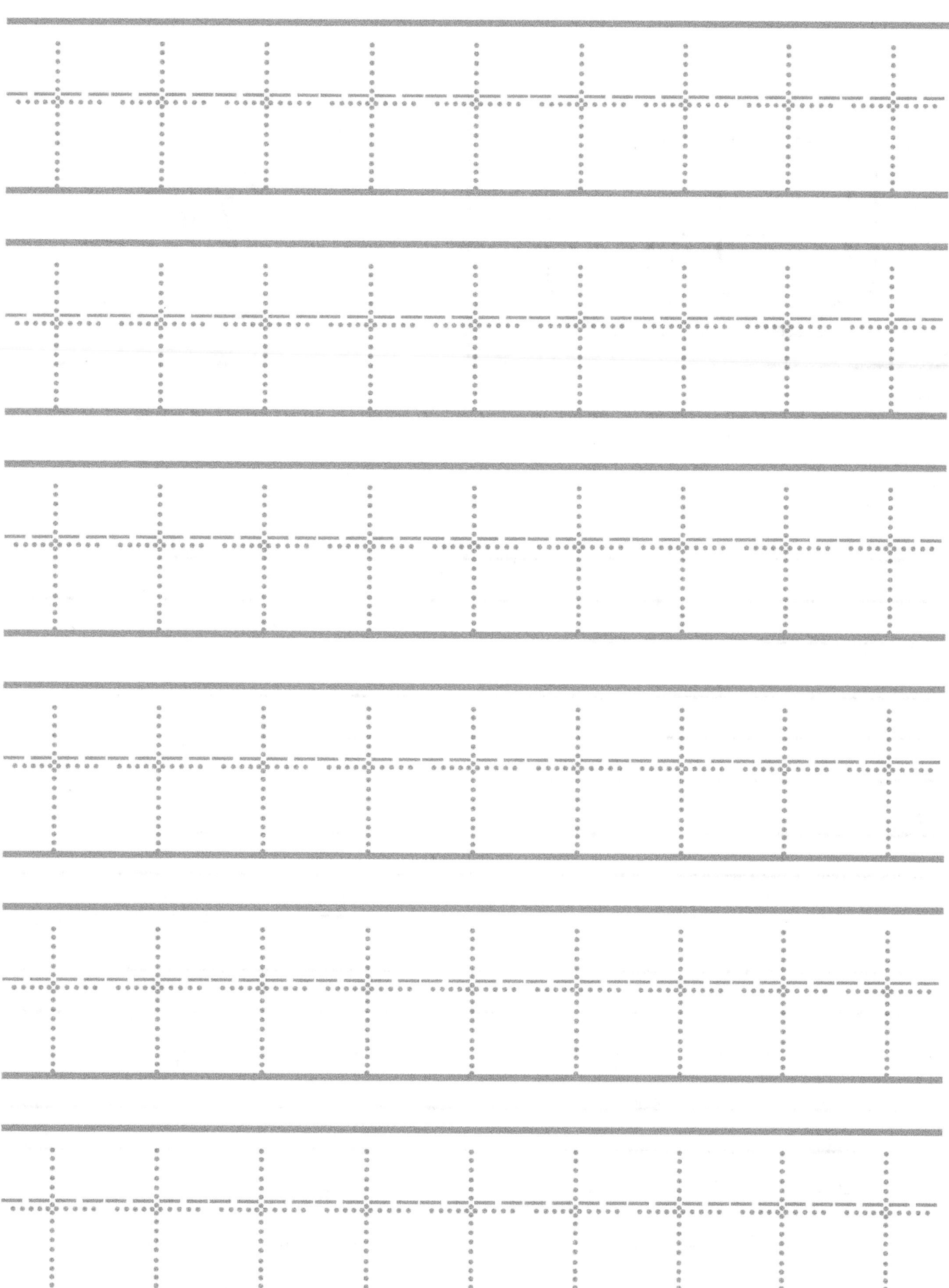

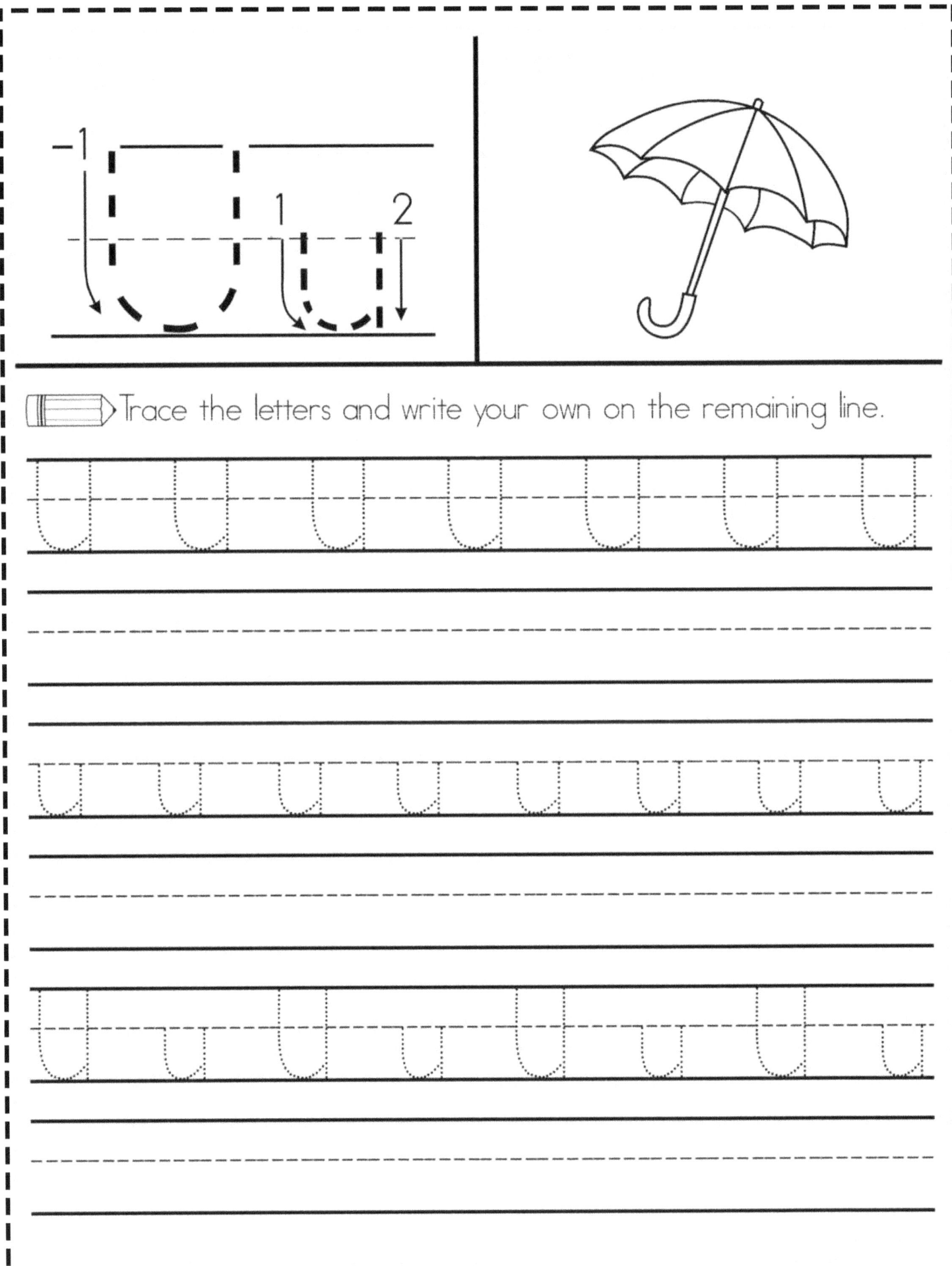

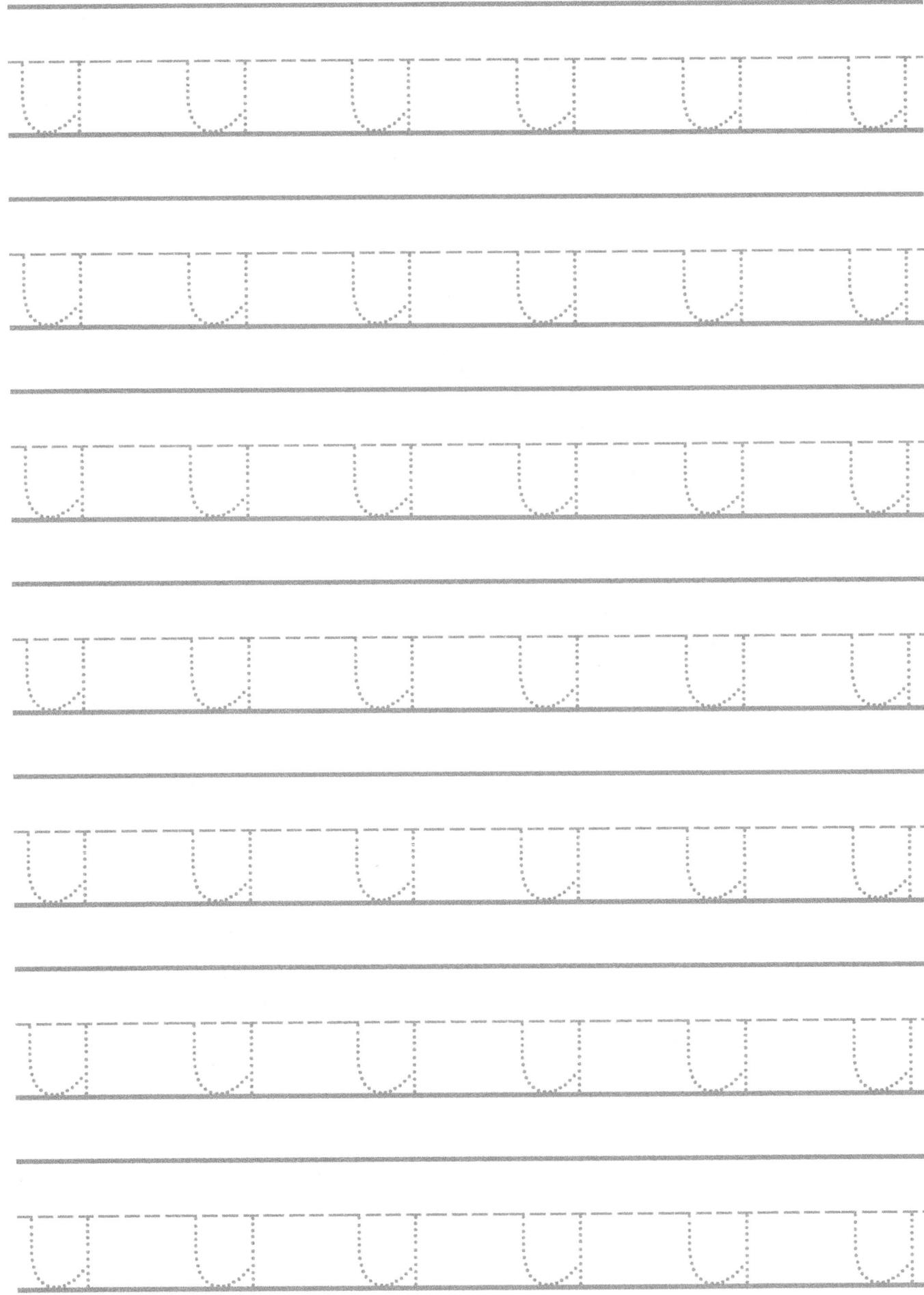

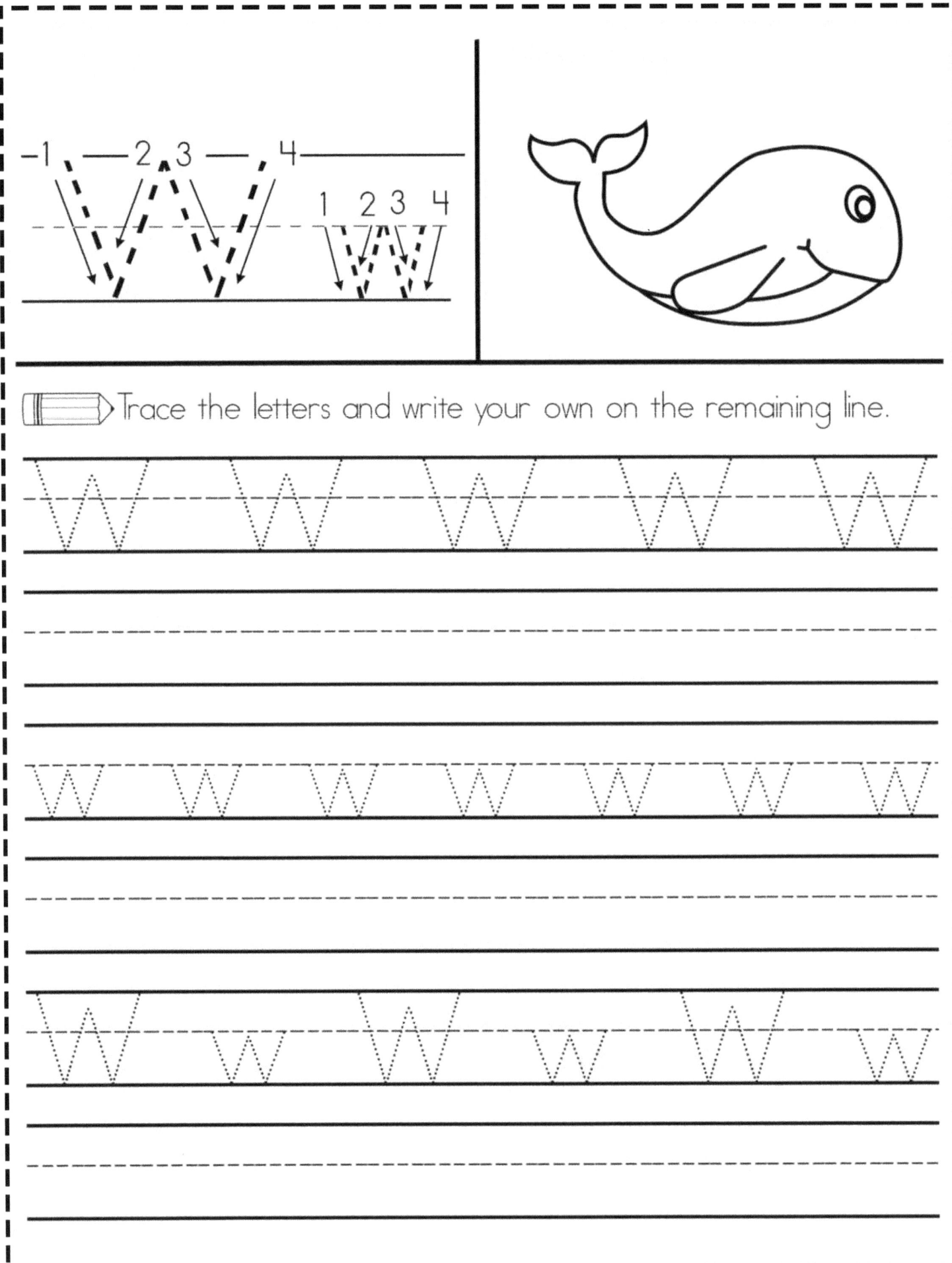

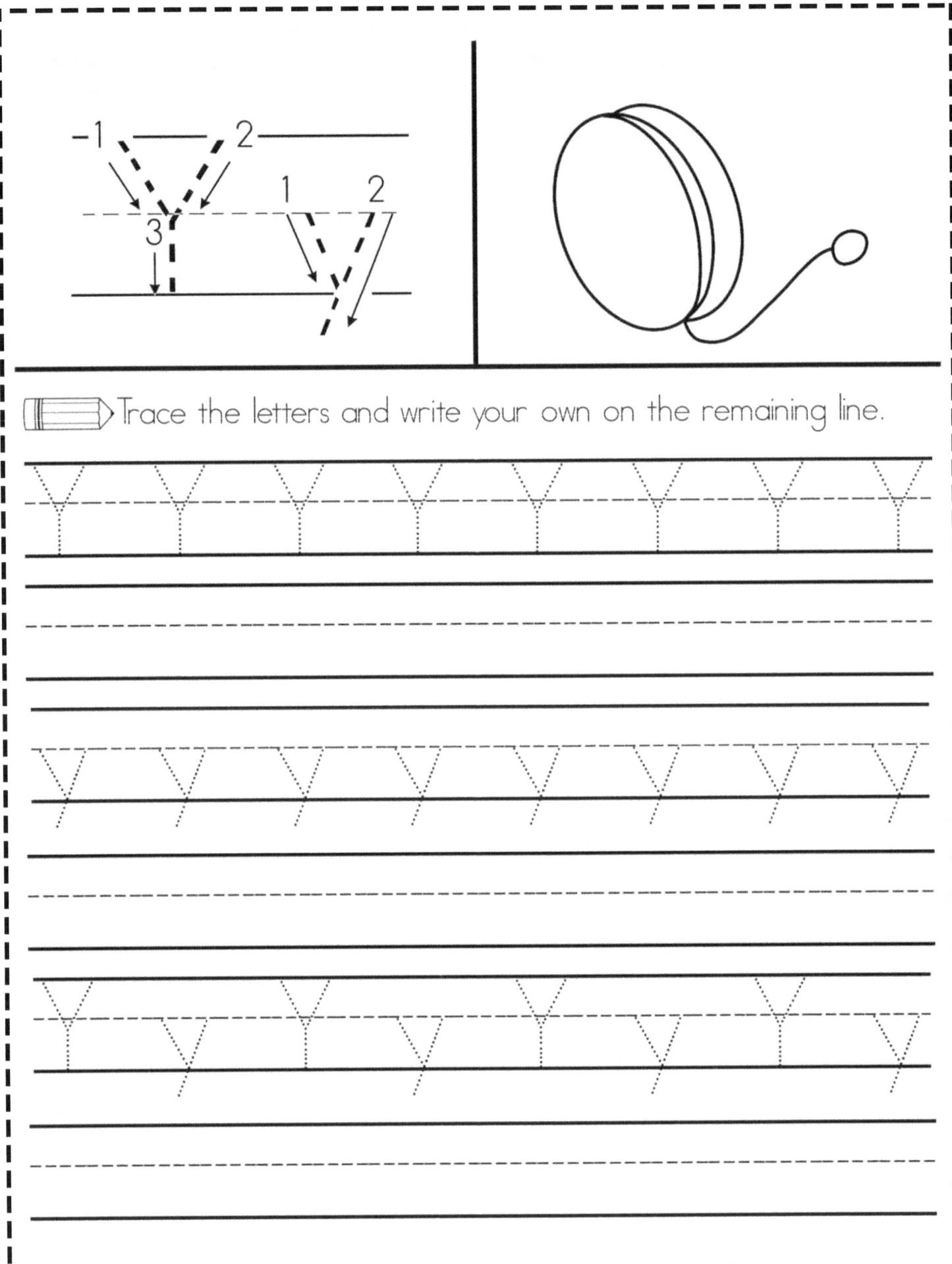

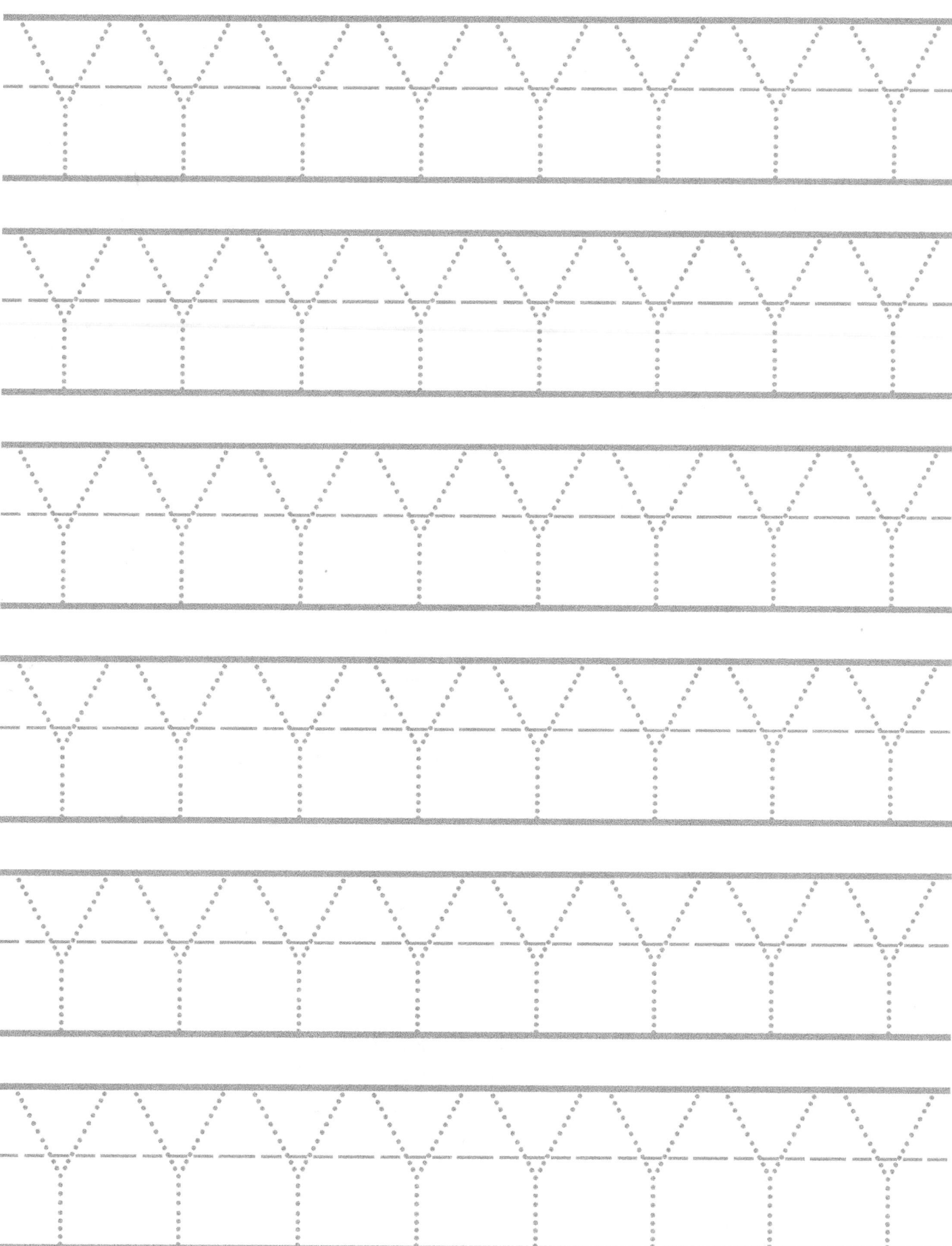

One One One One

One One One One

One One One One

One One One One

One One One One

One One One One

One One One One

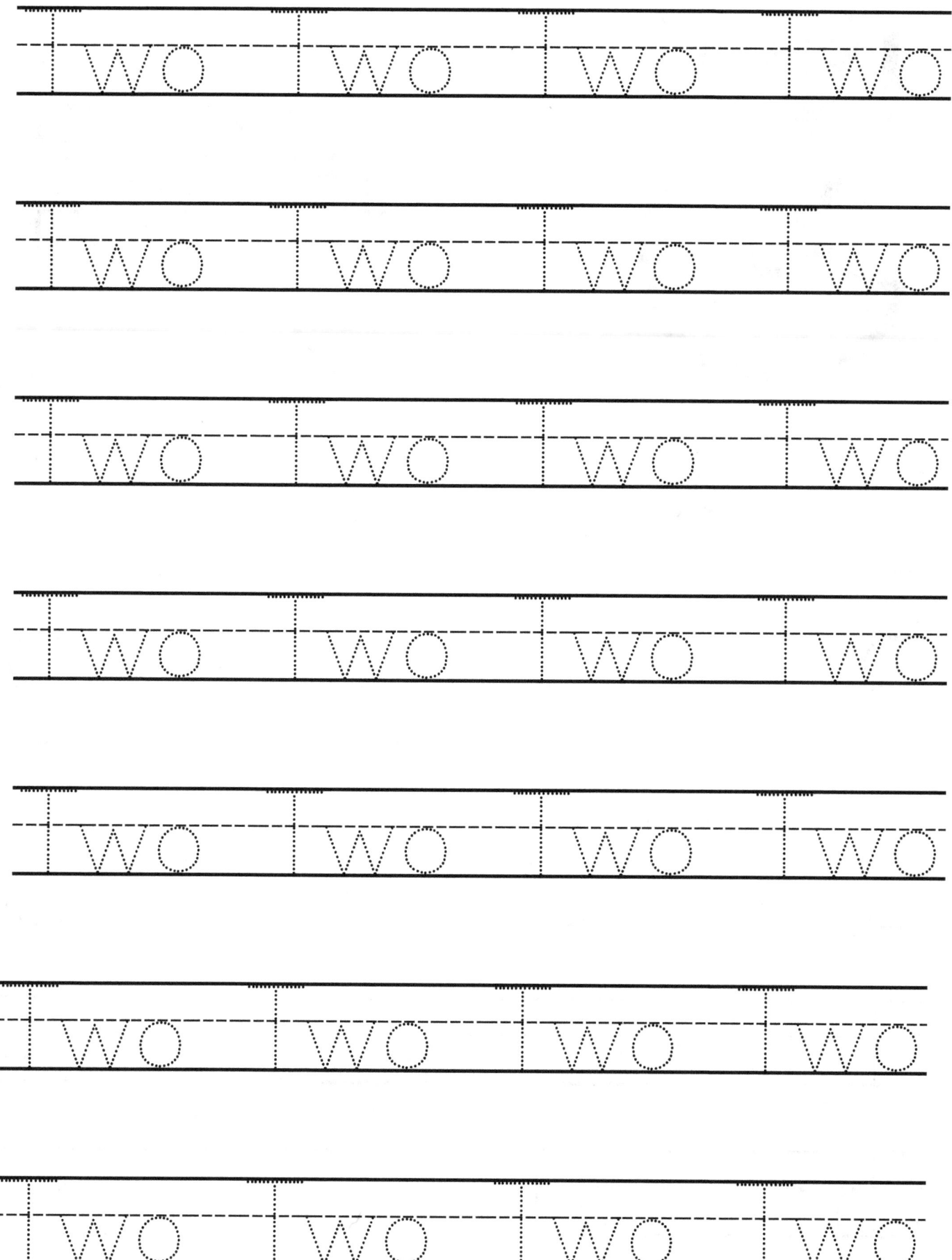

3 3 3 3 3 3
3 3 3 3 3 3
3 3 3 3 3 3

Three Three Three
Three Three Three

3 3 3 3 3 3

3 3 3 3 3 3

3 3 3 3 3 3

3 3 3 3 3 3

3 3 3 3 3 3

3 3 3 3 3 3

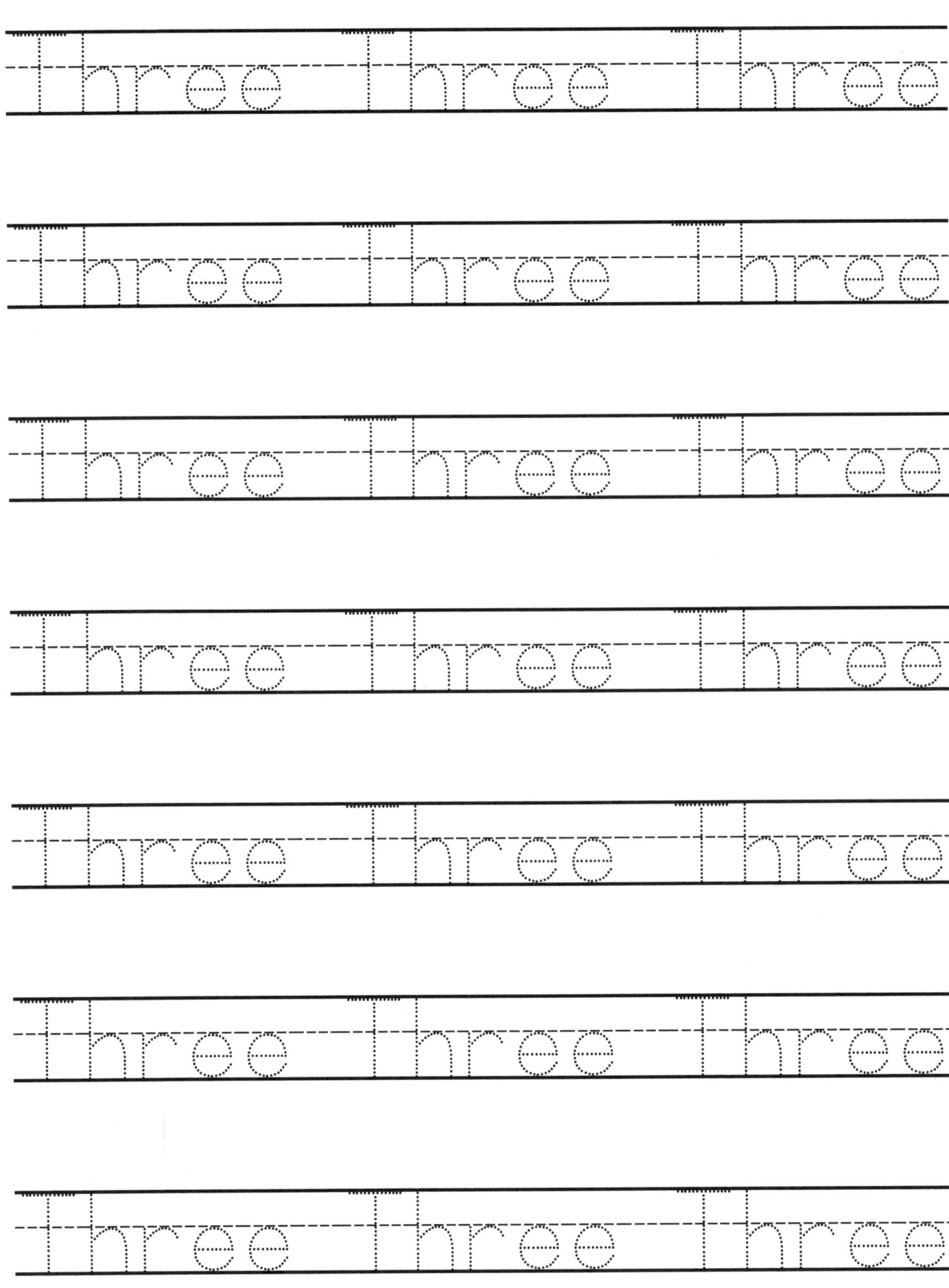

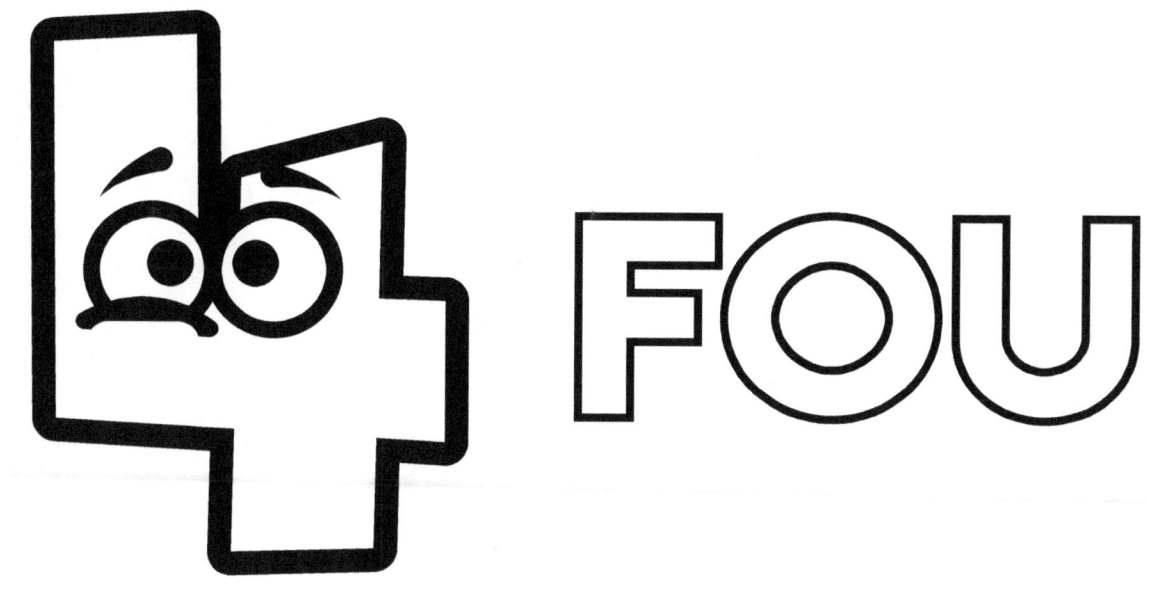

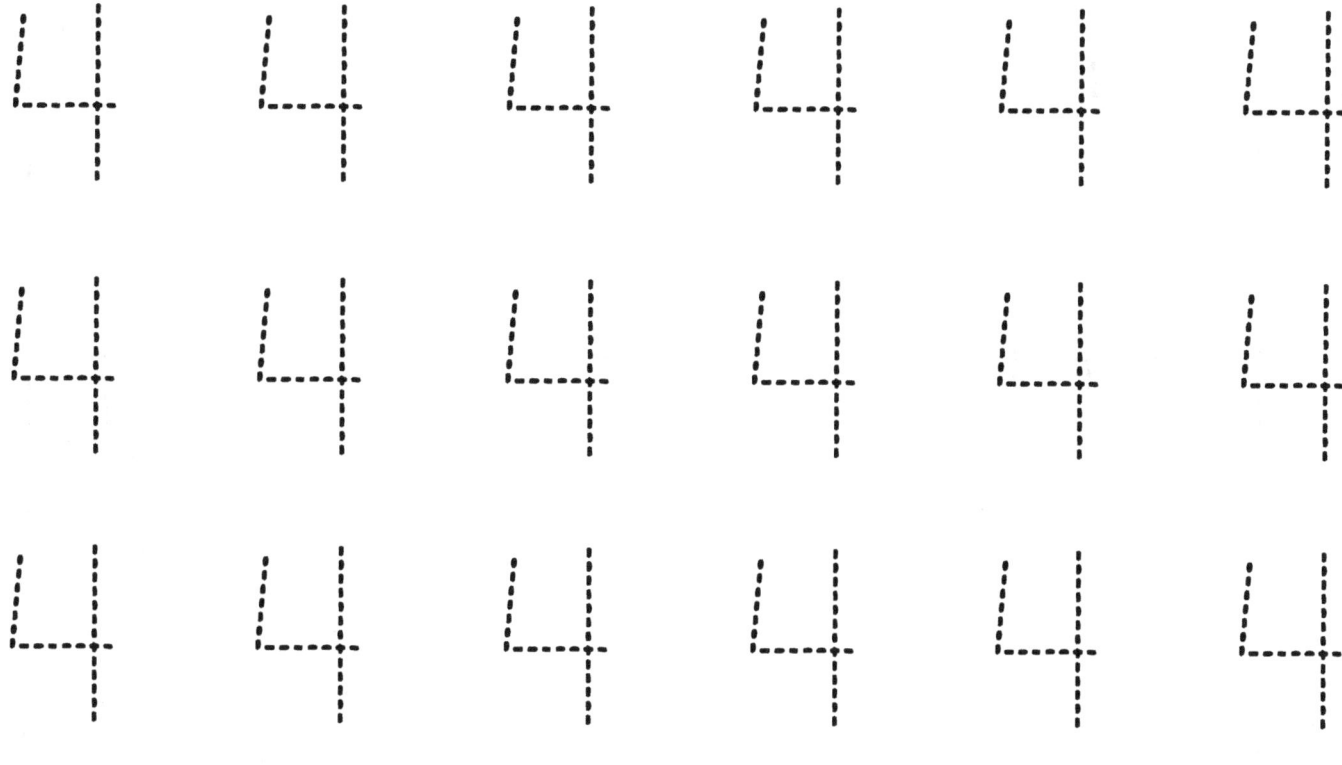

Four Four Four Four

Four Four Four Four

Four Four Four Four

Four Four Four Four

Four Four Four Four

Four Four Four Four

Four Four Four Four

5 FIVE

5 5 5 5 5 5
5 5 5 5 5 5
5 5 5 5 5 5

Five Five Five Five
Five Five Five Five

5 5 5 5 5 5
5 5 5 5 5 5
5 5 5 5 5 5
5 5 5 5 5 5
5 5 5 5 5 5
5 5 5 5 5 5

Six Six Six Six Six

Six Six Six Six Six

Six Six Six Six Six

Six Six Six Six Six

Six Six Six Six Six

Six Six Six Six Six

Six Six Six Six Six

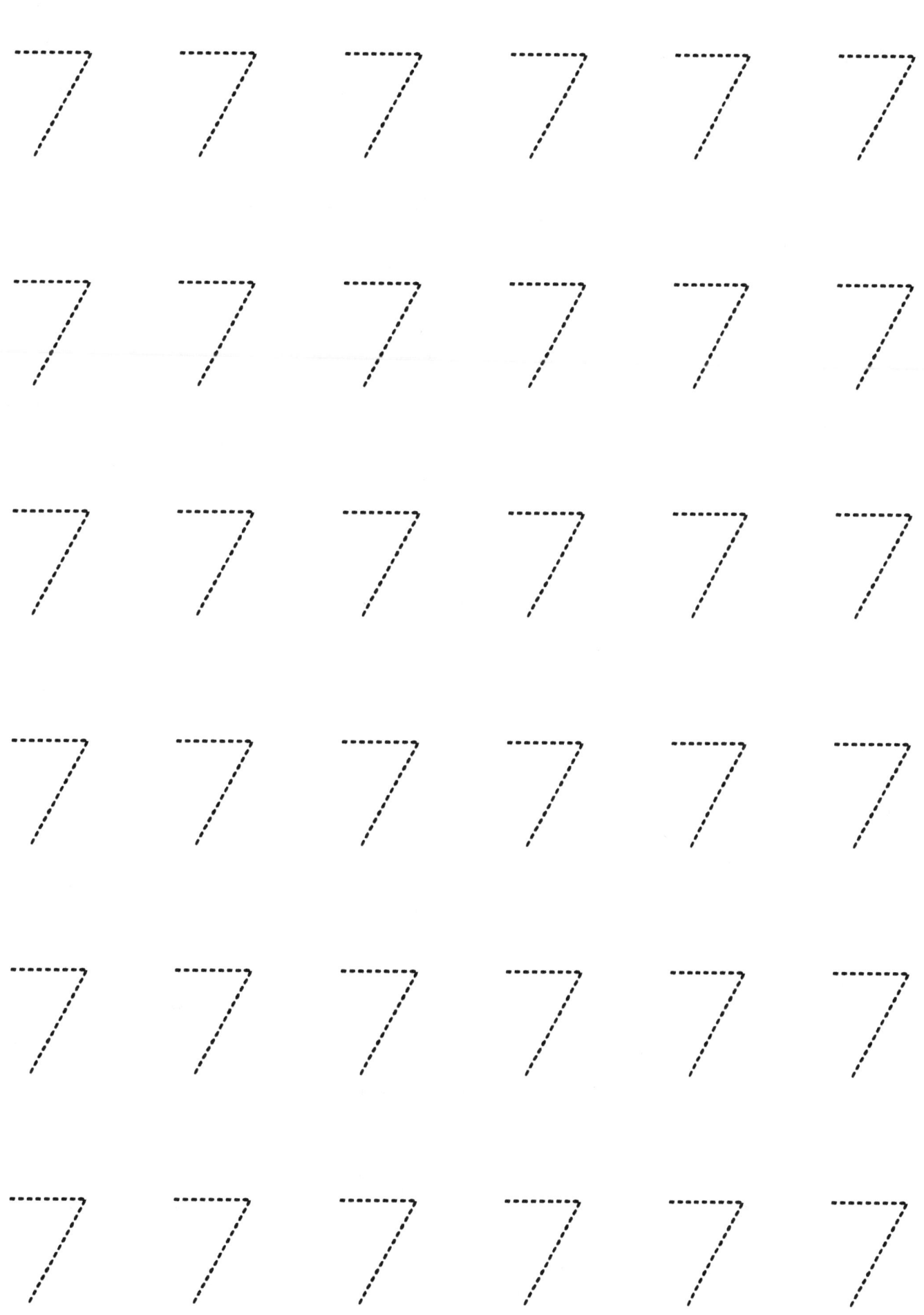

Seven Seven Seven

Seven Seven Seven

Seven Seven Seven

Seven Seven Seven

Seven Seven Seven

Seven Seven Seven

Seven Seven Seven

8	8	8	8	8	8
8	8	8	8	8	8
8	8	8	8	8	8
8	8	8	8	8	8
8	8	8	8	8	8
8	8	8	8	8	8

Eight Eight Eight
Eight Eight Eight
Eight Eight Eight
Eight Eight Eight
Eight Eight Eight
Eight Eight Eight
Eight Eight Eight

9 9 9 9 9 9
9 9 9 9 9 9
9 9 9 9 9 9
9 9 9 9 9 9
9 9 9 9 9 9
9 9 9 9 9 9

Nine Nine Nine

Nine Nine Nine

Nine Nine Nine

Nine Nine Nine

Nine Nine Nine

Nine Nine Nine

Nine Nine Nine

10	10	10	10	10
10	10	10	10	10
10	10	10	10	10
10	10	10	10	10
10	10	10	10	10
10	10	10	10	10

ten ten ten ten

ten ten ten ten

ten ten ten ten

ten ten ten ten

ten ten ten ten

ten ten ten ten

ten ten ten ten

www.ingramcontent.com/pod-product-compliance
Lightning Source LLC
Chambersburg PA
CBHW081014040426
42444CB00014B/3208